Never too Old for God

Margaret Cole wouldn't listen.
Even when they told her she was too old.
Widowed, children grown and married, she was
free to fulfill her lifelong desire to be a missionary. NEVER TOO OLD FOR GOD recounts the
incredible adventures that Margaret Cole experienced while serving the Lord in distant lands.
She witnessed astonishing miracles which God is
performing today, as great as any in the Bible.
Her exciting story just goes to prove that you're
"never too old for God."

Never Too Old for God

Margaret Rice Cole

as told to
Don Tanner and Bruce Anderson

Marshalls

Marshalls Paperbacks
Marshall Morgan & Scott
3 Beggarwood Lane, Basingstoke, Hants, RG23 7LP, UK

Scripture quotations not otherwise identified are based
on the King James Version of the Bible.

Scripture quotations identified LB are from The Living
Bible, Copyright © 1971 by Tyndale House
Publishers, Wheaton, Illinois 60187.
All rights reserved.

British Library CIP data
Cole, Margaret
  Never too old for God.
  1. Christian Life
  I. Title
  248.4 BV4501.2

ISBN 0-551-01250-1

Reproduced, printed and bound in Great Britain by
Hazell Watson & Viney Limited,
Member of the BPCC Group,
Aylesbury, Bucks

With deep gratitude to my beloved son, William; his wife, Linda; and my daughter, Charleene Stockdale, without whose help I could never have gone on.

My heartfelt thanks to my precious prayer partner, Dorothy Sims, whose encouragement was so vital, and to the Go Ye Fellowship missionary group, which adopted me into its membership.

In sincere appreciation to all those who faithfully upheld me in prayer.

Contents

Foreword
by Rita Nightingale

My first meeting with Margaret Cole was in the filthy surroundings of a Thai prison. She was every inch a sweet old lady, and I thought she looked incongruous in such a place, but I couldn't imagine why she had come to visit me.

She had come to tell me about a personal friend of hers — Jesus. I was not interested, being very angry and bitter about my twenty-year prison sentence, the treachery of my boyfriend who had planted heroin in my suitcase, and the injustice of it all. How could this old lady come and tell me about God's love!

But it was the beginning of a very special relationship with a remarkable woman. Even when I discovered the love of God for myself, and He began to take away all the hate and bitterness, Margaret's love was still a shining star to me and a continual encouragement.

The day I discovered she had written to the King of Thailand offering to take my place in prison and serve my twenty-year sentence was a real milestone in my Christian life. I knew that if Margaret could make that offer, knowing that she would die in prison if it was accepted, and yet seeing it as a means of serving God with joy in her heart, I could face it too.

Margaret Cole is an inspiration to *all*, young and old, and her example is a challenge to us to examine our own commitment to God.

April 1985

My Gift

What have I, Lord, to offer Thee—
A mind quick and alert,
Time for long-range plans ahead,
Wisdom, Thy truths to assert,
Preparational training for Thy work
Or skills or talents bright?
No, none of these are mine to give
I have only a widow's mite.

A life near spent, my only gift—
What a trifle for a King!
Oh, that I had a more worthy one
But such as I have, I bring
And offer it all. And may it, I pray,
Be acceptable in Thy sight;
Humbly upon Thy altar, Lord
I lay down my widow's mite.

MARGARET RICE COLE

1
Cannibal Valley

Exhausted after a torturous ride in our Land Rover—a trip which came to an abrupt end in a muddy ditch—I fell into a deep sleep in the heart of the remote Tirora village of Papua New Guinea.

Suddenly, the silent darkness burst with the sounds of terror. With eyes burning from the thick, black smoke of fires in the hand-thatched huts, I stumbled wearily in the night, trying to discover the reason for all the confusion.

It's a tribal war! The horrifying thought shot through my mind. In the next few moments, I would learn that about a hundred Wantaks from a nearby village had fled in terror to seek refuge here, having been attacked in the night by another tribe, which accused them of sorcery. Their village burned and their gardens destroyed, the Wantaks hoped they would be safe with us, and we had no way of knowing whether the enemy would pursue.

Events such as this are common occurrences among the people of Papua New Guinea, and I

15

was sent by the Lord to these citizens of the jungle.

As dawn broke over the dusty little native village, my hostess, Lois Vincent, decided it was safe enough to hike with her children through the surrounding lush green hills. With the sparkling water shimmering from a rushing river below us and the majestic solitude of the cloud-capped mountains above, we strolled along a flower-adorned trail, feeling like travelers suspended between heaven and earth.

The serenity of our meditation on the land's beauty was broken by a group of rushing warriors, armed with bows and arrows, dressed in grass skirts and brightly colored feathers, looking fierce with pig tusks thrust through their noses.

Escape From the Volley of Arrows

"Big war ahead," one shouted in broken English, eyes gleaming with the thrilling excitement of coming glories. Soon, the faint echoes of shouts could be heard cascading through the valley. As we stood apprehensively debating what to do next, a volley of arrows whizzed overhead. Suddenly, a small band of warriors swept by us in retreat. "We killed head man!" they shouted at no one in particular; a second volley whizzed overhead.

Grabbing the children, we ran up the hill to

escape, as more retreating warriors streaked past us. Gazing with fascination and dread at the combat scene below, we watched both sides in the battle as they danced and cast incantations at each other, their unearthly gutteral voices shattering the stillness of the countryside with curses at the enemy.

Courage fortified, they prepared for another attack. Suddenly, as if enraged by angry insults from below, the clouds opened, pouring torrents of steaming water on the warriors and the spectators lining the nearby hills. The monsoon rains had begun again.

Everyone scattered to escape the downpour. The war was over for today, a short retreat from an unbeatable enemy. The valley would soon see warring factions renewing hostilities, as part of the never-ending conflicts among the hundreds of tribes inhabiting this incredibly beautiful island paradise.

Hurrying back to our village, I breathed a prayer of thanks to God for allowing me to be a part of His mission to these people. I was helping to lift the veil of darkness from their eyes and to show them the good news of Jesus' love. Often we hear of happy, innocent peoples inhabiting these remote parts of the world, but my experiences there have shown me differently. Oppressed by evil spirits and sorcery, the villagers of New Guinea are gripped by fear, threatened at any moment by merciless attack. Within, I felt a heavy burden for these Stone-Age people, realizing that only the grace of God can deliver them from this life of superstition and violent, sudden death.

Did I fear for my safety in this different culture? You bet! A 71-year-old widow, I was apprehensive about living among such primitive people, some of them cannibals and headhunters. But my Father had made me a promise: "The angel of the Lord encampeth round about them that fear him, and delivereth them . . . . out of all their troubles" (Psalms 34:7, 17).

In extraordinary situations, God always brings extraordinary help. A few months after my experience, missionaries in the twenty-five-mile-long Ilugwa valley also found themselves in the middle of a war—this time directed against them.

Jenny Sexton was up early to feed her new baby when the peaceful silence of the morning was crushed by heavy pounding on the door.

"War in next village!" their houseboy screamed through the bolted door. "All Christians murdered. Now warriors coming here!"

Bonfires had been spotted in the valley the night before, but no one realized that spirit ceremonies were being held in preparation for war. Now, six separate groups of fierce fighters were converging on the tiny mission station, bent on killing everyone they found and destroying the radio and airstrip.

As the Sextons frantically tried to establish radio contact with the Bokodini base, the armies reached a nearby village to recruit more warriors. Mbajok, one of the village leaders, who respected the missionaries for their kindness and love, refused to join the fighters and sent relatives to defend the mission station while he rallied others to help stave off the attack.

The invaders continued their destructive march, burning villages in their path and axing men, women, and children to death while spraying arrows in every direction. Finally, Mbajok's men assembled to halt the juggernaut. A fierce battle ensued, as the enraged warriors threw all their might against these jungle brothers who would dare resist their advance. But the defense held, and soon a Missionary Aviation Fellowship plane swooped from the sky in response to the missionaries' desperate call. Bouncing along the airstrip, the plane rescued the Sextons, leaving the angry savages in the dust.

Defending villagers and Christians alike mourned their dead and nursed the wounded, deepening the friendly relations between them. God once again had turned evil into good, protecting His people and opening a passage through which the message of love could flow.

What is a woman my age doing in a place like this? This seems to be a common question, wherever I go around the world. As our airliner first arrived in the country, an Australian soldier sitting next to me shook his head in disbelief.

"Don't you know New Guinea is about to adopt self-government?" he stammered. "If you have any sense at all, you'll turn right around and go home. They expect this to become another Congo as soon as self-government is granted. The smart people have already left. I'm here to evacuate the Australians!"

Silently pondering his words, I reviewed my motives for coming. More than anything, I wanted to know the Lord in a more direct way and learn to depend on Him alone. Second, realizing how caught up I had been with material possessions, I wanted to prove to myself that things and money didn't really matter. Little did I know then to what extent God would honor my request on both these counts.

I had put down the first piece of a large jigsaw puzzle—my willingness to go anywhere—and now He was filling in the rest of the picture. Everything had fit with perfect timing, and I knew it was God's will that I be here, right at this moment. Independence or not, this enchanting land of lizards, bugs, scorpions, and mice was the place for me.

Beginnings

My mind raced back to Detroit and the closing years of World War I. A sawdust-floored tent was erected near our house, and I attended the children's Bible classes. That was when I first heard about Jesus Christ and how He loved *me*.

Coming from a non-Christian home, I had never heard Bible stories or much about God. I attended these Bible classes faithfully and proudly received a Bible for memorizing Scripture verses.

Near the end of the summer program, the children were asked to give their lives to Jesus, and I was among the first to respond. The love that I felt for God at that moment has never left me.

Soon after, my family moved to Chicago, and we lived near the Moody Tabernacle pastored by Paul Rader. Attending that sawdust-floored church, I sang in the girls' choir and formed and taught a Sunday-school class. I was committed to spreading the good news of Jesus everywhere, and had the joy of seeing many people surrender their lives to Christ.

I will never forget the day I was baptized by Pastor Rader. He asked if I would like to say something, and full of youthful enthusiasm, I announced, "I want to go to the mission field as soon as I can!" God filed that request away for more than half a century, but the desire never left me, and He never forgot it!

When our family moved to Denver, I was heartbroken to leave all my friends. Soon, however, I became active in the Salvation Army and later attended its training college in San Francisco.

Appointed an officer, I was sent with Lila Ward to open a new work in Redondo Beach, California, where I have lived ever since. The two of us would hold open-air street meetings five times a week, singing songs accompanied by the guitar and bass drum we played, and passing the tambourine for a collection. Some evenings the fog was so thick at the beach we could hardly see our audience, but God blessed our efforts and they began to grow into a substantial work, complete with a Salvation Army Hall.

Along with my other responsibilities, I had charge of our welfare work in the several cities which comprise the South Bay area of Los Angeles. Collecting old clothes and furniture, raising money before there was a United Fund, and feeding the needy, we worked long hours of heavy labor. Eventually my health failed, and I was forced to resign.

A short time later the treasurer of our Corps, Charles Cole, and I were married. We lived forty-five beautiful years together, a marriage founded on Jesus Christ and dedicated to His service. Raising a son and daughter, we were very dependent on each other and grew even closer after Charlie retired from the Redondo Beach Post Office.

During the retirement years, we traveled all
over North America in our trailer and also visited
Hawaii and the Caribbean. Those were such
happy times. After a few years, however, Charlie
broke his hip and was hospitalized. A successful
operation was marred by infection, and his condi-
tion deteriorated.

Charlie was bedfast, able to sit up only a few
hours a day in a wheelchair—at best. After two
years of home care, the doctor advised that a con-
valescent hospital be found for him. As Charlie
continued to fail, I prayed that God would do
what was best for Charlie. I would stay by his
side as long as he lived. The Lord became so
close to me in those final days before Charlie's
death, it was almost as though His arms were
around me.

Widowed now, children grown and married, I
was free to fulfill my lifelong desire to be a missionary. "Lord," I prayed, "I have only a widow's
mite to place on Your altar. I wish I were
younger, better trained, more talented—such as it
is, I give my all to You." To my delight, He took
what I offered.

I had heard that Wycliffe Bible Translators
would use people who were self-supporting, in
good health, and with usable skills as short-term
assistants in their mission work, so I applied as a
bookkeeper.

"Where would you like to go?" I was asked.

"Wherever the need is greatest," I replied.

"That's easy. Papua New Guinea!"

"Where in the world is that?" I asked. I would soon find out. There in "Cannibal Valley"—as some call it—I was to have my first brush with death.

Forgiveness, Not Payback

Bumping along in a small Jungle Aviation and Radio Service (JAARS) plane to the Wycliffe Bible Translators base at Ukarumpa, a song kept going through my mind: "Just when I need Him most, Jesus is near to comfort and cheer."

My heart was warmed as I looked down at the tiny villages nestled deep in the mountains below. Many of these people have never seen a white man or heard of a written language. In extremely primitive conditions, the Bible translators labor faithfully to create an alphabet and form a language, so the people can read God's Word. I was deeply honored that He would allow me to serve alongside these dedicated missionaries, sharing their joys and sorrows and relieving some of the crushing burdens of responsibility and overwork from their shoulders.

Descending into Ukarumpa, my new home, I was overwhelmed by the intense beauty of the country spread out below; an expanse of crushed green velvet, channeled by deep valleys and rivers wending among breathtaking mountain peaks. As we bounced onto the Aiyura airstrip, my heart trembled with anticipation. What had God prepared for me?

Ukarumpa is a base built by and for Wycliffe missionaries, who came from ten countries and a dozen denominations, and includes the two hundred support personnel who back the Wycliffe translators living in the far-flung villages. Tucked away in a five-thousand-foot high valley, the base is a self-contained city of dirt streets and busy people. Assigned as bookkeeper at the base store, I would release others to work in remote villages.

It didn't take long after my arrival to learn what a drastically different culture I was in. Here, strong family and tribal ties are everything. For an outsider to break those ties means death, often in tribal war.

On one occasion a young doctor was driving with a friend from Ukarumpa through primitive tribal areas to Goroka, the local administrative center. The road was harsh and treacherous, forcing the doctor into tight-lipped concentration as they jostled along. Suddenly, a small boy—one of the hundreds of villagers who constantly stream along the road—darted out in front of them. With no time to swerve, the car struck the boy with a sickening impact.

Ignoring frequent warnings never to stop in such a situation, the doctor and his young friend quickly climbed out of the car and ran to examine the child. He was dead. As the doctor held the small, lifeless form in his arms, a crowd gathered from the boy's village. Screaming and wailing in a threatening dirge, they began pelting the two men with stones. Unable to escape the encircling mob, the men collapsed under the vicious hail of rocks and were battered to a bloody death as they lay in the road.

The ancient demands of *payback* had been fulfilled. Tribes which have contact with the Christians, however, learn of a strange new custom: forgiveness.

Jackie Ruth was a vivacious, blond, high-school girl who worked with me in the base store at various times. Enjoying every day to the fullest, she brought many friends into her circle of happiness. Jackie also had a deep spiritual dimension to her life and had given it completely to the Lord, asking Him to use her as He willed.

On Good Friday, Jackie and her friends buzzed out for an evening ride on their motorbikes. The New Guinea army was holding maneuvers at the base airstrip, a thrill no young person would want to miss. The deafening roar of camouflaged military vehicles; planes diving, swooping, and ascending; the mock charges of troops; and the flares studding the black night sky held great fascination for everyone.

While they watched the display in excitement, an army truck, lights out, bolted suddenly out of the dark. With a shuddering crash, it rammed straight into Jackie's bike. She was instantly killed.

Gloom settled heavily over the Ukarumpa base that Easter weekend. Jackie's father, flown hurriedly home the next morning from a weekend assignment, was crushed with grief at the loss of his oldest daughter. Still, he said, "We gave her to the Lord when she was a baby. If He chose to take her home, that's all right with us."

That same spirit pervaded the Easter Sunday services. College students from Goroka and Kinantu, who camped outside Ukarumpa for the holiday weekend, joined in Jackie's memorial service. The evening found the students at her home, where they usually went after church for songs and fellowship. This day especially they felt they should be there.

The love of God overflowed in that home until late at night, and the day ended with more than thirty college and high-school students accepting new lives in Christ. Jack Ruth concluded, "God has changed my sorrow into joy," as he led one after another to salvation. That night the youth camps exploded with excitement, as the Spirit of the Lord settled on the students.

Soon after, Jackie's parents located the driver

of the army truck. "I expected you," he sighed
with resignation. "I killed your daughter, and
now you're entitled to payback."

"We didn't come to kill you," they exclaimed
in horror. "We love you."

"How could you love me?" he asked, bewildered at such strange words.

Listening to them explain the love of Jesus
Christ and how His forgiveness was projected
through them to him, a smile of relief grew on the
soldier's dark face. He accepted their gift of
Jackie's Living Way Bible and soon began reading it. Within a week, the army major requested
fifty more Bibles for his troops. Jackie's friends
collected the necessary money and joyfully presented the Bibles to the soldiers.

Because of the Christian version of payback,
many soldiers, students and villagers gave their
hearts to the Lord. Through her death, Jackie
Ruth had a great influence on the people all
around the Ukarumpa base.

The mountains of New Guinea hold a great
hunger for God. The culture is pervaded by
thoughts of the spirit world, but the spirits are
enemies of the living. Those who have heard the
message of Jesus and His power over evil are
overwhelmed by its implications, never seeming
to hear enough about His love and forgiveness.
And the change in a tribesman's life when he
becomes a Christian is impossible to miss. When

an occasion demands payback, it is replaced with forgiveness, just as Jackie's father practiced it. This was the greatest miracle I saw in New Guinea.

The Spirit of Power

Some villagers are so consumed by the Gospel message that they want to preach it everywhere, with or without training. One weekend I was invited to a graduation ceremony at Christian Leaders Training College, where many young men were about to depart for the jungle as pastors and evangelists among their people. This ten-year-old school, nestled in a lush green valley surrounded by towering peaks reaching to sixteen thousand feet, teaches dedicated young men how to preach the Gospel.

During my visit, I was shocked to learn how these pastors and their families survived on only a few dollars a month. Even in New Guinea, inflation takes its toll. Feeling I had to do something, I asked principal J. Oswald Sanders to select one young man whom I could help support. Because of his busy schedule, he forgot to get back to me. Turning to the Lord, I asked Him to point out the right one.

Graduation night came, and one student after another filed up to the platform to speak of his love for Jesus and his call to the ministry. When

Sibala Waleba prepared to speak, I knew immediately he was the one. The father of several children he had left behind in their village, Sibala was already a pastor but wanted to learn more about the Lord.

He revealed how his children had not been cared for as he was promised when he left home—at one time they were living on grasshoppers—and I felt an overwhelming urge to give him my support. After the meeting, his dark face grew radiant as I offered to help buy food and clothing for his family. To this day, Sibala is actively working for God as a full-time pastor. It is a wonderful feeling to help support such a dedicated man of God.

The Bible translators are equally dedicated to the Lord's work, spending years in isolation and hardship to spread the Bible's good news.

One cloudy day a busload of us from Ukarumpa sat on a grassy hillside with people from the Gahuku village, waiting anxiously for a long-awaited event. Translator Ellis Deibler was escorted by the village's Catholic priest to a crudely made platform, on which rested a stack of newly printed Bibles.

Hands shaking with excitement, Ellis triumphantly held one of the Bibles—the first translated into the Gahuku language—over his head. He and his wife had lived fifteen years with the tribe, facing loneliness, discouragement, and frustrations, to develop their tongue into a written language and teach the villagers to read the Bible in it.

"The work is finished!" Ellis shouted exuberantly. "Come, get your book." As if in response to his words, a shaft of sunlight suddenly pierced through the mass of clouds overhead and beamed directly upon the upheld book. Tears of joy streamed down our cheeks as it seemed God Himself had turned on a spotlight from heaven, approving the work done in that remote, hidden village.

More of these rays of light are desperately needed to drive out the darkness that pervades rural New Guinea. In a culture of spirits and sorcerers, only the full power of the Holy Spirit can transform lives. And when the Spirit is there, the changes are awesome to behold.

Near Ukarumpa base lies the village of Gadsup, the home of an old sorcerer who has given his life to Jesus. Because he no longer practices sorcery, tribespeople appeal to the new sorcerer when illness strikes. He concocts magic potions and performs frenzied spirit dances, but his powers are pitifully useless. Finally, they turn to the old Christian, who prays to God for their healing. As many of the sick are healed, knowledge of the true God spreads.

One weekend when I was visiting this village, a *sing sing* was held late into the night. Members

of an adjoining tribe had cast a sorcerer's spell on
one of the men from the village, and the villagers
believed he had died as a result of the spell.

Dressed in war paint and armed with bows and
arrows, eyes gleaming with demonic hatred in
the flickering glow of their fires, they danced far
into the night. Suddenly in their midst appeared
three young Christians—like the three Hebrews
walking into Nebuchadnezzar's furnace—and the
sing sing lapsed abruptly into silence.

As the hush fell on the warriors, they stared in
awe at these young men who would dare inter-
rupt. Sensing a superior power radiating from
them, no one moved as Maru, a twenty-year-old
who had recently given his heart to the Lord,
spoke quietly about the love of God. "Your spirits
have no power," he concluded. "Turn to the real
Spirit of power."

When he finished speaking, the warriors
looked quietly at the ground, then one by one
shuffled back to their huts. The sing sing was
over; no revenge would be taken. God's irresisti-
ble love had conquered the evil spirits, and
peace was restored in the Gadsup tribe.

No one working in the jungles of New Guinea
can doubt the strength of Satan's power, but he
also knows it falls helpless in the face of a committed Christian. ". . . greater is he that is in
you, than he that is in the world," the Bible says
(1 John 4:4). It would not be long before I would
have to test this firsthand.

2
The Hut of Humility

Please help us!" I pleaded to the crowd of by-
standers as the small but powerful warrior pulled
me toward the jungle. My scalp tingling with
fright, I tried hopelessly to struggle free of his
iron grip.

Just a few minutes before, Pastor McCarthy
from Sydney, Australia, had been taking several
of us on a leisurely drive down a dirt road toward
the New Guinea village of Kudjip, when the warrior stepped abruptly out of the bush to meet our
car. Brightly regaled in war paint, wearing a brilliant headdress of bird of paradise and cassowary
feathers, with long tusks through his nose and a
cowrie-shell necklace on his chest, the bushman
seemed friendly enough, so we decided to stop
and take photographs.

After a few pictures, he gruffly demanded
money. His face had knitted into a fierce frown.

"We don't have any money," we tried desperately to explain. But it was no use.

With an angry grunt, he grabbed Mrs. McCarthy and fumed, "She be number-one wife." Not

satisfied with her alone, he then took hold of me, muttering, "She be number-two wife."

My imagination ran a close race with the wildness of the warrior now dragging me toward an unknown destiny. In a flash of realization I could see it all: me, the wife of a scantily clad savage, planting gardens, digging yams, and carrying heavy loads on my head for the rest of my life. A large, hostile crowd gathering at the roadside began to slowly press us toward the bush, away from our car.

"McCarthy," I yelled, "give him your pen!" When that failed, he tried offering his tie, then his shirt. Nothing worked; the warrior wanted money.

Just as we were about to disappear into the jungle, Joy Nicol, a lady who worked with us in the store at Ukarumpa, called out in excitement. She had discovered two shiny dimes in one of her pockets, and they were offered hopefully to the tribesman.

As we held our breath, praying he would accept the ransom, he grabbed the coins and abruptly dropped us, stalking back into the bush.

The fearful incident has now become a joke. Twenty cents, and I was only the number-two wife! Friends keep sending me quarters to help pay my next ransom, and I have had an inferiority complex ever since! But it wasn't very funny at the time, bringing home to me the vast gulf separating us from the culture of rural New Guinea.

Many times I visited villages, sitting with the women and children while they took turns stroking my hair in delight. In a land of wiry-haired people, my head seemed to be adorned with the strangest headdress. On one occasion, I was wearing a wig. A small boy stroked too hard, and the hairpiece came completely off my head. Shrieking in horror, he held my "scalp" in his trembling hands, sure a worse fate than he could imagine now lay in wait for him! The crowd of children ran away in fright, until I showed them my hair could be put back on. Then they were enthralled and followed me everywhere.

My nylon stockings, too, were fascinating to the villagers. Calling them "rubber skin," they took great delight in pulling out the stockings and watching them snap back, to the accompaniment of giggles all around.

Meals were quite different from what we are used to. On a visit to the Rawa tribe at Tauta village, I was invited to spend the evening with several of the villagers. Sitting on the dirt floor around a fire pit, we passed the evening with friendly conversation, periodically reaching in and taking something out of the big, black cooking pot that dominated the small hut. As we ate whatever our fingers dredged out of the pot, I managed to force a friendly smile of appreciation

at the warm community spirit of these primitive
people. I also asked the Lord for more than just a
blessing on the food! Another time one man, who
made the mistake of asking what the meat was,
hurried outside the hut and was violently ill. The
meat was rat.

Once the native language helpers came to dine
with us, and I cooked a large dinner for them.
They had never sat at a table or used forks and
spoons before, but like us, they were gracious
enough to eat everything set before them, including all the butter and the last drop of catsup. To
leave anything on the table is considered an in-
sult to the host.

God gave me a genuine love for these people.
His love spans the gulf of race, culture, and language, supplying a universal communication that
can be understood without ever speaking a word.
Just as Jesus broke the bread to feed the mul-
titude, He broke my heart in love and sympathy
for these bush people, so much in need of the
Bread of Life.

I came to realize that, in spite of the great dif-
ferences between us, we are united by common
needs and desires. The tribespeople of New
Guinea want shelter and warmth, food and water,
just as we do. It doesn't matter that their homes
are thatched huts with dirt floors, or that their
hair is smeared with pig grease. They possess the
same love we have—the same hate and sin, too.

While their wars are on a smaller scale than ours, their deaths are just as real. Like us, the ultimate need of these people is spiritual, a void that can only be filled by the love of Jesus.

Our God Will Move That Rock

When the Christian faith spreads in an area dominated by demonic spirits, struggles are inevitable. Once, in one of the villages where missionaries were working, the chief arrogantly challenged God.

"Our spirits have great power," he boasted. "Your God—weak. If He so great, have Him push down big rock on hilltop."

The missionaries took up the challenge. God was not to be mocked, and His power would not be denied. After a period of intense prayer, they sensed God would support them.

"Our God will move that rock," the leader announced boldly. "But we will give your spirits an opportunity to do it first."

With the demand for success now upon them, the chief's warriors began their spirit dance with frenzy, thumping on the graves of their ancestors and wailing their spirit flutes throughout the night.

The rock did not move.

Now it was up to the missionaries. They began to pray. That night, a sudden tropical rainstorm struck with full force. Rain pelted the hilltop, pounding with great fury. The next morning the villagers huddled together, and as they looked up the hill, the huge rock suddenly lurched and rolled down, not stopping until it reached the bottom. With a final crash, it split in half as the awe-stricken villagers watched. As in the time of Elijah before the priests of Baal, God had not failed His people. The spirits were discredited, and a new spiritual wind blew gently into that village.

In another tribe, a young man had just become a Christian, and this made the village sorcerer furious. "You will die at midnight," he intoned threateningly, and the man ran in terror to the missionaries who had led him to Christ.

"Don't be afraid," they reassured him. "God's power is greater than Satan's. Jesus defeated the evil powers on the cross, and they have no more authority over you. You are surrounded by protection."

At midnight, the young man was on his knees with the two missionaries, praying fervently to the Lord for deliverance. The hour came and went, and still the young man was in perfect health. God had protected him from the worst evil he could imagine; now his faith leaped to new heights.

Yet death *had* struck the camp. The next morning the village sorcerer was found dead.

"Jolly Margaret"—Miserable?

Such first-hand reports stirred my faith to the point that I was ready for anything from God. I knew He was faithful and that His power was superior. But still times came when discouragement pressed on me like a heavy weight. I had many lessons of faith yet to learn.

In the early days of my stay at Ukarumpa, I was surrounded by a dense cloud of depression. Others had experienced the same problems, caused by the satanic spirits remaining in that ancient valley. Having always been an excellent sleeper, I now found myself waking a dozen times during the night, short of breath from the high elevation and longingly thinking of home.

During one Saturday-night prayer meeting— when everyone was supposed to tell how joyful they were in the Lord—I sobbed loudly, "Well, I'm not happy. I'm miserable!"

Shocked by such an outburst from "Jolly Margaret," they placed me in the center of a circle and prayed. It didn't seem to help a bit. Later, alone with God, I realized that I had come here to know Him better and to rely on Him alone. How could this be accomplished without hardships? My faithfulness was all He asked of me. Was that too much to expect?

In shame and repentance, I asked for forgiveness and deliverance. Soon, I sensed God's peace driving out the depression.

All along, I had thought the Lord and I would be laboring together on the mission field, but as it turned out, He was doing the working—on me.

My Fall From the Palace of Pride

One day our store manager said longingly, "Wouldn't it be great if we had a walk-in refrigerator? These old freezers and iceboxes became antiques years ago."

"I'll write a check for a new refrigerator," I said, rising to the occasion. It was quite a tidy sum. My excitement building, I told a few friends, who spread the news of what I was buying. The refrigerator would stand as a monument to my generosity and ability to provide for the base. I would be set apart from those around me, who had to depend on others for financial support. People would say, "There's Margaret Cole. Look what she's done for the Lord."

I was soon brought down from the palace of pride to the hut of humility. In a direct hit to my soul, God showed me the dedication of these missionaries at Ukarumpa—brilliant, educated people serving Him in the Stone-Age bush, unable to write a check for even the smallest amount.

I met a pilot who had given up a brilliant career with a major airline to hop over the jungle in tiny

THE HUT OF HUMILITY

planes. Then, observing our base doctor, I realized he could have been a wealthy man back home, yet he lived his days serving hundreds of needy people, diagnosing illness over a shortwave radio and receiving an embarrassingly small salary.

I recalled Ellis Deibler, who has a Ph.D. from the University of Michigan and degrees from Fuller Seminary and Columbia. Out here he is translating the Bible for a tribe of villagers unknown to the rest of the world. I also thought of Ernie Richert, a brilliant, educated man who worked seventeen years to translate the New Testament for the Kipu village, singlehandedly bringing there water, electricity, printing facilities, and small shop industries in the process.

Pierced by the horror of my self-satisfaction, I cried to God for forgiveness and went immediately to the base directors. On their advice, my donation was redirected, this time anonymously, and for the first time, local villagers were hired to help translate the Bible into their own languages. A refrigerator would have only broken down someday, I concluded, but the lives touched by God's Word will last for eternity.

Soon another lesson in faith came my way. Experiencing deep pain in my abdomen and doubling over, unable to straighten up, I finally forced myself to visit the base doctor.

"You have an acute gall-bladder infection,

N. O. F. G.—3

Margaret. You must go to the hospital at Goroka," he ordered. "They'll confirm the diagnosis. Then, if you're smart, you'll fly home for surgery."

Fly home? After the Lord sent me all the way over here? That didn't sound like God's will. If surgery was necessary, I resolved, Goroka would have to be the place for it.

Since no transportation was immediately available, I painfully endured two more weeks of working in the store, meanwhile praying for my healing. Barely able to eat and after losing many pounds, I finally could stand the agonizing pain no longer and drove with another missionary to Goroka.

Tests verified my fears: gall-bladder surgery was indeed required. But even at this point, I was enveloped in a supernatural peace. With or without surgery, God was still in charge. I surrendered it all to Him.

Final examinations were run the next day. Dye test, fatty test . . . . And just then, God healed me! By the time the nurse had reached the X-ray stage, my pain was completely gone, and no stones were visible! A repeat of the earlier tests indicated a perfectly functioning gall bladder.

"You don't need surgery," the doctors agreed after a surprised consultation. "Pack your bags and go home. Your gall bladder will probably outlast you!"

Excited and praising God, I left Goroka the next day. But not until after eating a huge celebration dinner with friends, just to prove my healing. The Lord had brought me through my strongest test of faith yet, and had done it in triumph.

Back From the Beyond

Dosi, a woman from the Gadsup tribe, also knows the faithfulness of the Lord. Soon after delivering her fifth child, Dosi suddenly collapsed at the door of her hut. Discovering her cold, limp body there, Dosi's husband, Tom, lifted it to the bed and called for Samoke, a Christian friend. Samoke and his two sisters, also Christians, ran into the hut and examined her: no heartbeat, no breath—just a terrible stillness.

Samoke and his sisters laid their hands on the lifeless form and prayed.

"Dosi," Samoke called earnestly, "you have many children, and you must not leave them. You must come back!"

There was an immediate response. The woman's body gave a slow heave, and deep gasps of air filled her lungs, transforming fatal stillness into the rhythmic breathing of deep sleep.

"Dosi alive again!" The news spread throughout the village. After three days in a local hospital, she was ready to return home. The Gadsup tribe knew they had witnessed a miracle.

When she regained consciousness, Dosi told this story:

I died—finish, true. I walked about in a place no good. Everywhere the big bush and kunai grass came up, and there was no road. I was lost and very frightened.

Then Samoke prayed and a good road came up and I walked on it, and I was very happy. I was not afraid any more.

After I walked on it a long way, I saw four watchmen on the road, and they stood aside for me to pass. A long way I walked, and I saw a house. Oh, it was a good place, true. It was a long house, very light—bright inside and out. Outside I saw eight watchmen, and one big man made nine. Their dress was altogether white, but the big man's dress was different. It was white, too, but very bright, and light was shining through it. It was very wonderful. His dress was down to his feet.

The eight watchmen stood aside and I went close to the big man. He spoke to me. "Why are you here? There is no place ready for you. The table is not spread for you. Your name is not here. Why have you come? I will come to your place, but you cannot come here. You are not ready. Go back to your people and talk to them all. Talk in the church. Talk in the village. You must not hide any of the words. Talk out to all the people."

In a simple and most beautiful way, He explained to her quite briefly the Gospel message: Who He was, why He came to Earth, why He allowed wicked men to kill Him.

"See where they nailed My hands and feet to the cross and where My blood ran down? Because I had no sin, I was able to take all the sin of the world. I took the punishment of sin. Nobody needs to carry his own sins any more. All can put their trust in Me. Now you must go and take the words to your people."

Dosi first told this to Tom, then to the whole village. Wherever the story is repeated, many lives are changed. Today, Dosi is still faithful to Jesus, and Tom has become an active Christian, too.

I Learned to Depend

Many are the stories and events I encountered during my time in New Guinea. Like a ray of brilliant sunshine, God's power shone through all of them, and I found a new closeness to Him. Whatever my needs—shelter, transportation, food, challenges, and tests—all were provided, and I learned what it means to be totally dependent on the Lord and the certainty that He is always true to His promises.

I also learned the reality of Satan, as well. So real and frequent were his temptations that they became easily recognizable. Nearly every month provided a new reason for going home, a new threat that had to be overcome. In a way, it was exciting to encounter Satan's temptations, because that meant my once-nominal Christianity was actually being transformed into a threat to the world of darkness. At times, the battles almost exceeded my limit of endurance, but to stand as God asks of us is a triumphant experience I'm glad to have known.

The materialism I had asked God to remove was often my means of trial. Reading part of a newspaper sent from home one day, I learned that the stock market was falling. I grew uneasy about my certificates resting uselessly in a safety-deposit box, and an inner voice seemed to say, *Go home and cash your stocks before they fall any more. You can give the money to the Lord.*

To make matters worse, I learned that a medical clinic was buying the block on which my house stood. If I were the last to sell, the value of my property would plummet.

With my worry at a peak, a thought from

heaven seemed to still the inward turmoil. *You came out here to prove that possessions don't matter. Now you have a choice—faithfulness or material gain. Which will it be?*

When it's put that way, what can you say? Asking the Lord for strength, I resolved to choose faithfulness, letting my investments back home take care of themselves.

It is now several years later, and my stocks have regained their value. Plans for the clinic changed, and the value of my property has skyrocketed. God doesn't want to deprive us of prosperity. He only wants our hearts devoted to Him alone.

With that difficult lesson completed, I was ready to learn total dependence on the Lord— and would soon experience it, during one of the toughest situations I have ever faced.

3

After the Incredible Earthquake

The long winter night was in its quietest hours, and I slept warmly bundled against the piercing cold of the Guatemalan mountain air.

The steady creaking of the old house that formed part of our missionary medical clinic kept time with my shallow breathing, as if in protest against too many years of freezing and thawing. Tonight, not even the symphony played by the antique water pipes could disturb my peaceful slumber.

Suddenly I was awake, feeling like a reluctant passenger on a ship pitching and rolling in a churning sea. At first not comprehending the deep roar coming from the earth, a flash of insight revealed what was happening.

"It's an earthquake!" I muttered in amazement. As the fearful shaking increased, my bed rolled back and forth across the undulating, shuddering floor, while I gripped the bed frame for support. Suddenly, the din intensified and the water tank outside spilled its contents onto the heaving earth with a roaring splash.

Despite the noise, peace filled my heart. It seemed as though the Lord was standing by my bed, assuring me everything was all right. As the shaking diminished, I congratulated myself for coming through it unscathed. "Well, that's about enough," I said with relief.

Just then, the main earthquake hit, pounding the walls like an enraged jackhammer. Whatever had been loosened by the first tremors was now crashing down. All I could do was pull the sheet over my face and pray.

In a mere thirty seconds, the devastating quake sent 23,000 Guatemalans into eternity, injuring three times that many and destroying the fragile adobe homes of more than one-sixth of the population.

None of us realized the extent of the damage until reports slowly trickled in from around the country during the next few days, revealing the worst disaster in Guatemala's long and calamitous history. Our district came through with relatively mild damage, although we lost twenty people and two hundred were injured.

A grim sense of numbness gripped the tiny country. With devastation everywhere, the nation joined in an anguished wail as thousands searched through the rubble for their loved ones.

Motherless children wandered the streets, while the lucky ones who still had families huddled together in makeshift tents of blankets, pieces of brightly colored plastic, and even cardboard cartons.

Panic grew as waves of aftershocks kept alive the memories of that terrible night, making a return to the quake-damaged buildings unthinkable. More than a thousand of these tremors struck in the month following the earthquake, hampering the intense efforts to rebuild houses before the imminent arrival of the rainy season.

Throughout the crisis, our little clinic kept going, serving and loving the people who had so little to lose, yet lost everything. Since the hospitals were bursting with victims, we received many of their patients. Our clinic could hold no more, but still they kept coming, and we kept taking them.

Dodging rubble and huge fissures in the road, we delivered soap, flour, sugar, and material for rethatching roofs to the outlying areas near the city of Tecpan, stirring up so much dust we had to wear masks. Feeling overwhelmed by the devastation, I didn't see how this country was ever going to rebuild.

A city of 25,000, Tecpan was left with only two buildings standing. The rest was huge piles of boards and mortar, under which moaning victims were still pinned. Those lucky enough to return unharmed to their homes often could not determine which street they had lived on. Tecpan was flattened.

Such experiences were common. A young father was kept alive by his children, who trickled water down through a hole in the rubble until help arrived two days later.

A fireman dug a woman out of a collapsed apartment house, only to find his own mother dead inside.

A mother and her children were saved by the strength of a bedstead, which shakily supported the weight of the fallen roof.

As always, the disaster brought out the best in people and forced them to face the realities of death. Many of those who had never given spiritual matters a thought were led to Christ.

In the plaza of the capital city, a large banner was raised, proclaiming that "Jesus is coming soon!" Hundreds began studying the Bible in small and large groups, perhaps realizing for the first time how tenuous a grip they had on life.

Juan Ruyan, a short, unassuming man of sixty-nine, was badly bruised by falling clay roof tiles. As pastor of the church in Patzun, which was totally destroyed by the earthquake, he needed all the help he could get. Still, when a missionary group handed him two hundred dollars to help rebuild, he hobbled slowly back to give them his tithe. "Here's twenty dollars," he said quietly.

"Use it for others who have need."

It may seem strange that God would send me to Guatemala then. Perhaps He intended to give me some advanced training in dependence. I *had* asked Him to test my faith.

"I'd like to know how much faith I've really got," I had prayed. On a base in New Guinea, I knew the Wycliffe people were there to help. "Take me somewhere new, to do something I don't anticipate," I had asked earnestly. "Let me discover how deep my love for You really is."

The Lord took me at my word. Given a much more difficult assignment than New Guinea, I learned again that His strength is sufficient.

God's Coincidence

Just before leaving for Guatemala, a letter came from Edith Moser, who had heard of my trip from a mutual friend. She had worked in the Mam Clinic. Edith described the appalling conditions there. "What a forlorn place that must be," I marveled, tucking the letter away, intending to forget it.

When I arrived in Guatemala City, I had no idea where God wanted me, so I went off on my own. Speaking little Spanish, I immediately met problems. I wanted to visit the Aurora Zoo and showed a map with a circle around the zoo to the bus driver. Soon all the passengers discussed heatedly where I should be let off the bus.

Here comes the revolution, I said to myself.
While the passengers grew louder and louder, I
escaped out the back door of the bus.

A man on the street directed me to the "right"
bus; it took me back to my hotel. The zoo
seemed to be a difficult place to visit!

I had similar problems when I asked for directions to a chicken restaurant. Asking for *pollaid,*
instead of the Spanish *pollo* (chicken) I was
shocked when the proprietor sold me a pack of
Rolaids! "Well," I figured, "maybe the Lord
knows I'll be needing these."

On Christmas Eve, I attended an English
church service and afterwards was left all alone
on a dark street corner. Waiting in vain for a bus
to come, I became frightened. "Lord, I need Your
help!" I prayed.

Almost immediately, some Americans arrived and asked me about buses. "There aren't
any here," I replied, greatly relieved by their
presence.

"They're still running on Avenida Reforma,"
one man joined. "Let's go back."

I knew my prayer had been answered. We
walked back, got on the same bus, and rode to
within four doors of my hotel. God's protection is
the best I know.

Before long, I volunteered my time for work in
a Bible bookstore, spending several weeks there.

When efforts to obtain a mission assignment met with total failure, I began to wonder if perhaps God wanted me at that clinic after all, and I asked the store owner about the place.

"Never heard of it," he frowned thoughtfully. "But there's a man from up in that area who comes here for supplies about every six months. I'll ask him next time he comes in."

"Six months!" I moaned. "I'll never get up there!"

No sooner had the words left my mouth than that very man strolled into the store. "Why, here is Mr. Rance now!" exclaimed the store owner in disbelief.

"Sure, I know the clinic," Alver Rance responded cheerfully to my shaky questioning. "In fact, we're driving up there next Sunday. You're welcome to come along if you like."

Hurriedly concluding the arrangements, I excused myself and ran into the back room to cry. God's coincidences are sometimes just too much to take calmly.

That Sunday the Rance family and I happily drove the four hours to Quezaltenango, enjoying the scenery as we snaked around narrow mountain roads to the clinic. Ruth Wardell the director was not there, having gone to the United States for a visit over the holidays. After seeing the desolation of the place, I was glad she wasn't.

"I don't think this is quite the place for me," I

announced sheepishly. To my surprise, Alver readily agreed.

"It's extremely cold in this high elevation," he said. "You'd be isolated—no one speaks English except Ruth, and she's always busy—and this volcano is always throwing out ash. I'll take you to our place, and tomorrow you can ride the bus back to the capital."

At that moment the inner voice of the Lord flashed into my consciousness. *You asked Me to test your faith,* He said. *Now you can know just how deep it really is. You'll go to the edge of physical discomfort, but no further. Do you believe My strength is sufficient? Think back; was it just coincidence that brought you here?*

With a shudder of sorrow at my wavering faith, I called to Mr. Rance. "Bring the luggage back. I'll leave it here until I find out if Ruth Wardell wants to use me," I said with more firmness than I felt. She wasn't due to return for a week, and maybe God would only ask for my willingness to stay. In any case, my stake was driven, and my heart was at peace.

The following Sunday, Ruth's jeep was parked outside as I went to church in Guatemala City. Just returned from the States, she had planned to go directly up to the clinic. "Yet for some reason," she said after I introduced myself, "the Lord kept me here an extra day. And *you're* the reason!"

I had kept administrative health files at a hospital in California, and Ruth had just lost her chart-file clerk. She was wondering where to find another one when God miraculously brought us together—she needing help, and I needing *to* help. What a marvelous life faith brings!

I was given the lower floor of a two-story adobe house at the clinic, complete with kitchen and bath. The days were exciting, but I had to spend the evenings alone in my quarters. Ruth devoted her evenings to writing reports and studying the charts of the day's patients in a solitary room across the clinic compound from me. Although sorely missing the Christian fellowship back home—the church services here were in Spanish, which I couldn't really follow—I realized this was what I had asked for, and it brought me one step further along the road of faith and dependence on God.

Something Unexpected

The Clinica Evangelica Mam is situated in the middle of a vast sea of cornfields farmed by the wretchedly poor Mam Indians. The surrounding green hillsides, dotted with flocks of sheep and spread with a colorful blanket of wildflowers, hold innumerable little adobe villages in which the Indians live, unhampered by the 8,500 foot elevation. The distant mountains sparkle in the clear air, interrupted here and there by the ugly, charred cones of volcanoes which break up the green beauty of the pines like gateways to hell.

Tight against a small, forlorn hill, called the "witches' mountain" for the sorcery practiced there, stands the clinic. Here, a mile and a half down a dusty—often muddy—road from the nearest bus stop and ten miles from the nearest store, Ruth Wardell, a short, energetic woman, does an incredible job of serving the Mam Indians. Her job consists of examining, diagnosing, prescribing, dispensing medicine, and delivering babies, as well as raising financial support and directing the staff of seven Indian helpers. A registered nurse, she has performed this remarkable feat for the past twenty-six years and has no intention of stopping. On my arrival, Ruth showed me the waiting room used by the patients during the four days a week of the clinic's normal operation. Here, in a small chapellike room, they sit on rows of benches and hear of Jesus Christ from Pastor Don Candelario. Those showing interest are visited later at home, and all who can read are given Bible portions in their own language.

Ruth pointed out the examining room where I would be working, a tiny cubicle lined with medicine cabinets and drawers for patient files. I was horrified to learn that my chart-filing work would be done standing up in that room, a scant arm's length from the examining table, which

held patients suffering painful injuries and
wracked by dreadful diseases. Still, God had
brought me here, and I was sure He would sup-
ply the necessary strength.

The one hundred to one hundred and fifty new
patients we saw every week—who, along with
return-visit patients, total more than eleven thousand each year—leave the clinic the same way
they arrive: walking if they are well enough,
otherwise being carried in homemade wooden
wheelbarrows or on a chair tied to someone's
back. That was our ambulance service. If they
must stay overnight, the patients sleep in a building across the yard, on solid-board beds. The family usually supplies gunnysacks for a mattress
and old clothes for a pillow.

One man spent a week there, literally stoned.
He was in traction for a back injury, and all we
could do was hang heavy rocks from his ankles
over the bed. The treatment worked, though, and
he left feeling fine.

As Jesus told us to "let our light shine," the
Mam Clinic is a lighthouse of the Gospel in that
isolated land. Physical help is given to the needy
and spiritual help is offered to all who will accept
it. Knowing they will not be turned away, patients stream in from early morning until dark.
Hundreds have found the Lord, with exuberant
joy flooding their lives and glowing on their
faces.

Although delighted for the opportunity to serve

in God's work, I would never have selected a clinic as the place to do it. When I asked the Lord for something unexpected, He certainly took me up on the request.

Avoiding sick people whenever possible, I had always dreaded hospitals. Just the sight of blood made me ill. Now I was standing less than three feet from patients groaning with injuries, suffering convulsions, terrible hemorrhages, wounds requiring stitching, and every other type of case imaginable. I helped deliver babies (twenty of them in one memorable month) and helped prepare the dead for burial.

After the earthquake, I was up all night with people dying in agony from their injuries, trying unsuccessfully to shut out the dreadful sound of the families wailing outside. My family back home was frantically trying to contact me; they were almost ready to fly down to Guatemala. But a missionary ham radio operator finally got through and told them I was all right. During this ordeal, I became fully aware of God's powerful support. I'm not a nurse, and I did not feel called to serve the sick, but whatever there was to do, God enabled me to do it. I knew I was where the Lord wanted me. That, at least, was unmistakably clear.

Dependence on the Lord

The clinic, too, was founded on dependence. Shortly after my arrival, Ruth called all of us at

the clinic to spend half a day in prayer for it. The
electricity had been off for several days, the
water pipes were broken, and we had only $2.14
on hand to meet an urgent bill for $200.

Kneeling on the hard cement floor for prayer,
our knees thoroughly chilled by the cold, we saw
God honor our faith. By afternoon, the water was
flowing, the lights were back on, and the day's
mail had brought a check for exactly $200 from a
supporter in the United States! The twelve of us
marched arm in arm around the clinic buildings,
singing praises to God! How could I doubt His
willingness to provide everything we needed,
after such a miracle?

The clinic has had an impact on many areas
of the Mam Indians' lives. Ruth calls on local
village homes, giving shots for measles and
whooping cough to the children, thus reduc-
ing the annual deaths from hundreds to almost
zero.

We often visited the dusty villages dotting the
countryside as part of our program of education
and evangelism. Learning skills of farming and
crafts, the Mams are trying to break out of their
poverty. It hurt me to know how despised these
warm and hospitable people are by the rest of
their countrymen.

"Oh, she's just a Mam Indian," a hospital official once told us when denying use of a life-

saving kidney machine to one of our patients. Yet the Mams know the meaning of love and how to welcome strangers.

It was a pleasure to visit their small adobe houses, covered with grass-thatched roofs, or galvanized metal roofs for the "wealthy." Invariably we would be welcomed into the single room by a smiling, barefoot family. As the children—dressed as small replicas of their parents—hid shyly behind their mother's dark wraparound skirt, the father, wearing only homespun cotton pants and a shirt, would graciously offer the meager fruits of his labor to the guests: perhaps some tortillas and beans, and on rare occasions, meat. All was cooked in the bare front yard, and there were never any leftovers.

Because of this meager diet, many of their babies are born with harelips and cleft palates. We worked patiently to keep them alive with special-nippled bottles and sometimes with intravenous feeding. Once a year, a dedicated doctor came to perform surgery on these children, correcting their deformity.

Prayer Cures Witch Doctor's Curse

One day an Indian mother timidly brought her child for the surgery over the threats of the village *brujo*—the witch doctor—who swore he would cast a spell of death over the little boy.

With a mother's perseverance, she insisted on the surgery, in spite of her very real fears for her son's life.

After the operation, the stitches kept pulling out for no reason and had to be replaced. The next day, a creeping paralysis grew over the tiny body, and the boy was soon unable to stand. Spreading to his arms and face, the paralysis prompted Ruth to rush him to the hospital in town.

On her return, she summoned all of us to prayer. "This is the work of Satan," Ruth announced ominously. "It can only be defeated by the higher power of God."

We prayed earnestly for an hour. Meanwhile, at the hospital ten miles away, the boy's paralysis began to fade slowly, the same way it had come—legs, arms, and face. Before long, he was speaking and eating again, soon returning to visit us, completely well. How our faith grew after this incident!

Strange Dedication

One day Ruth told me to jump in the jeep and come with her to a dedication. *It must be a new church*, I thought as we careened along the worst road I've traveled. Arriving at a village high in the mountains, we sat with a large group of people under a canvas covering, waiting for the ceremonies to begin.

A group of school children sang, a government official spoke, and a doctor we knew delivered a long address—all in Spanish. "What are we dedicating?" I finally asked Ruth, unable to contain my curiosity any longer.

She pointed to a tiny building in the distance. "But that looks like an outhouse!" I exclaimed in disbelief.

"That's exactly what it is," she laughed. "We're dedicating two hundred and five of them!"

The clinic's young helpers, called "health promoters," circulate throughout the isolated villages, giving instruction in good health habits and nutrition, along with the Gospel. They had convinced every farmer in the area to build an outhouse, and we were dedicating them that day. *God works in mysterious ways*, I thought. Jesus told us to meet physical needs, and sanitation is an important ministry, too.

Mams Rejected by Their Brothers

One of my constant prayers was for God to give me a deeper love for these people. The Mam Indians, once proud descendants of the ancient Mayans who ruled Central America, have been left behind by the Spanish-speaking progressive elements of Guatemalan society. Reduced to poverty and hopelessness, the Mams cling to life

in the farmed-out lands of the mountain high-
lands, victims of malnutrition, disease, and a religion full of fearful spirits that must be placated by
animal sacrifices and black magic.

Willing to give anything to help lead these
wonderful people out of their despair, I became
close to them as I bumped along in the over-
crowded buses, traveling several times a week to
Quezaltenango. After trekking a mile and a half
to the bus stop, I would be crammed into the
lumbering old bus and squeezed between any
two people who seemed to have an inch to spare.
Often, I found myself suspended in midair over
the aisle—held in place only by the pressure of
those on either side of me. No one ever fell out of
these aisle seats; they defied the laws of gravity!

The smell was almost overwhelming as the
dirty bus rattled noisily down the rough road, but
somehow it didn't dull my affection for these
people. As chickens and squealing piglets wandered under the seats, fruit and vegetables from
the Indians' baskets bumped and spilled
everywhere. A mother with an extra baby would
automatically put it on my lap, making me wish
they had heard of rubber pants. It didn't really
bother me, though, and I was able to help many
of them find the Lord.

When the love of Jesus fills these Mam Indians, no Christian anywhere can outdo them in
spiritual graces. Having already learned the

hardest lesson—how to be humble—they trust the Lord totally, as only the helpless can.

During my stay, the church in the little town of San Juan, cultural center of the Mam Indian district, had a crisis. The fifty-odd Latins in the congregation decided to throw out the five hundred Mam Indian members, calling them dirty, illiterate, and lower class. Although such accusations were not new to the Mams, they certainly didn't expect them from their Christian brothers.

"What shall we do?" they asked one another at a hurriedly assembled meeting.

"We outnumber them ten to one!" responded one of the younger members. "Let's throw *them* out!"

"I think we should appeal to the presbytery," suggested an older man.

"Brothers," an elder said firmly, "let's get on our knees and ask the Lord what we should do."

They prayed long hours and searched the Bible diligently for a solution. Many of them had found Christ in that humble church; they had been married in it, brought up their children there, and centered their lives on it. Leaving would be a terrible loss to these destitute people.

But God's will was clear. "We will leave," they announced to their Latin brothers, without a trace of bitterness. "We do not wish to dishonor Jesus. God will provide. We will make do."

My heart was as saddened as theirs when they

walked slowly out of their beloved place of worship. The greatest cruelty of all is when your own brothers reject you, as Jesus Himself well knew.

Going to Dave Scotchmer, the missionary who had brought so many of these people to the Lord, I asked if anything could be done.

"Their offerings totaled only three hundred dollars last year," he replied glumly. "They couldn't buy anything with that."

"God won't let them down," I insisted. "Have them look for another place. Somehow, He will provide."

After a thorough search, they found a crumbling old building nearby, which the owner offered to sell for $6,200. He wanted $1,000 down, which of course they did not have. Suddenly I knew another reason why God had sent me to the Mam Clinic! I gave a promissory note, and the building was secured.

Upon my return to the United States, I told this moving story at a local church, and its board voted $3,000 to help buy the building. A few additional donations were raised, and the full $6,200 was soon obtained. The Mams now have a debt-free building of their own in which to worship.

Knowing what it was to be rejected, Jesus had honored their Christian humility. For the first time, they have something that really belongs to them. Their joy overflows—the offering has leaped from an average $6 to $100 a month. Prayer vigils are being held every night, and the congregation has already outgrown the building. It is obvious to me that the Lord's faithfulness always exceeds ours, and His love is given without measure.

Once I learned what it's like to live on faith, any other life-style became intolerably dull. But life in the coming months was to be anything but dull.

4
Thailand Triumph

"No one is allowed into the camp," growled the guard, lifting his rifle threateningly. Behind him stood a crowd of wide-eyed Cambodian refugee children, watching eagerly as we tried to enter this forlorn camp in southeastern Thailand.

"But we have Bible literature and lessons to give out," pleaded Alice Compain, my missionary companion who had served in Cambodia before its fall. "Can't we talk to someone in charge?"

With a grunt, the guard pointed to the administration hut where the provincial director of refugee camps was visiting. Encountering difficulty in entering camps in Thailand was nothing new to me, and I was sure of God's leading. My unmistakable mission was to help comfort the Christians imprisoned behind these barbed-wire fences. But how? While Alice talked with the officials, I was startled by a definite inward impression from the Lord.

Go on in! The words flashed into my mind.

"I can't climb over the barbed wire," I protested, "and there are soldiers blocking the entrance. I could never get in."

Just walk in, continued the impression.

"All right, Lord," I whispered. "Here I go."

Where Grown Men Weep

Looking straight ahead and determined, as if knowing what I was doing, I strode boldly past the guards and headed down the dusty main street of the camp. To my amazement, no one tried to stop me. It was as though an invisible hand had blinded their eyes.

I immediately began searching for an English-speaking Cambodian who could lead me to one of the Christian leaders. Because this camp lay so close to the Cambodian border, the area near it was threatened by frequent attacks of the invading Khmer Rouge; all missionaries had been pulled out of the area by their sponsoring organizations. I wanted at least to have a brief time of fellowship with the Christians here, before I was forced to leave.

As I walked down a lane in the camp, the Christian leader spotted me and assumed I was with a Christian organization. Speaking broken English, he introduced himself and led me to the other believers. We gathered in one of the tin-roofed longhouses for a worship service. Here, families are crowded into tiny cubicles ten feet square, separated from others by only a sheet or blanket strung halfway up to the ceiling. Lacking furniture, we sat on the bare wooden floor where the refugees sit, eat and sleep amid scattered piles of personal belongings.

These refugee camps house many Christians converted during the great outpouring of God's Spirit on Vietnam, Cambodia, and Laos before their fall to the Communists. As American troops held back the advance, missionaries redoubled their efforts and had a great harvest of people who are now largely in refugee camps.

I taught a Bible lesson from the Epistle of Peter:

> God has reserved for his children the priceless gift of eternal life; it is kept in heaven for you, pure and undefiled, beyond the reach of change and decay.
>
> These trials are only to test your faith, to see whether or not it is strong and pure. It is being tested as fire tests gold and purifies it—and your faith is far more precious to God than mere gold . . . .
>
> 1 Peter 1:4, 7 LB

My heart choked with emotion as we sang together to the music of a broken old guitar. In a camp where grown men weep because they have little food to give their children, where small boys and girls sit with tin cans at the bottom of a well to catch a trickle of water, these Christians are steadfastly serving the Lord, refusing to blame Him for their plight. I could almost see their shining faces as they will stand before God's throne in heaven, clothed in dazzling white, purified as fine gold.

The situation is the same in Thailand's thirteen other camps, which host a population of more than 100,000 that grows daily. Having a long border with Thailand, Cambodia supplies many of the new refugees, who escape daily from the cruel grip of the Communists, to crowd the already overflowing camps.

And still they keep coming, straining an already weak Thai economy to the breaking point. To these victims of boredom and malaria, a hopeless life of imprisonment in a refugee camp is far better than the fate of the one to two million of their countrymen who have died since the Communist takeover. Stories told by refugees have a chilling similarity—forced marches, inhuman cruelty, and vengeance on a scale unknown to Americans.

Two brothers told me of their twenty-nine-day flight from Cambodia through the jungle, subsisting on bamboo sprouts and dew collected on leaves. Yet that was preferable to a life of terror in their homeland, a bare existence of starvation, rampant disease, and scarce medicine.

I was reluctant to leave these beautiful people—famished for fellowship, eager for a sponsor to help them out of the camp—but Alice had received permission only to hand out Bible outlines and then leave. "We'll see you in heaven," we said with all the joy we could muster, as we walked slowly back toward the main gate.

The Mysterious Escape

A stream of wounded Thai soldiers coming in for medical attention filed past us as we left. The Khmer Rouge had invaded that border of Thailand. Their advance was being checked only two miles from the camp. Soldiers ran everywhere in preparation to meet the soon-expected attack.

"What now?" we asked each other. With the road closed to traffic, the bus we had expected to take back to the city would not be coming. It was already dusk, and we were many miles from the nearest town. With the sounds of gunfire echoing in our ears, we sat down at the camp entrance, ignored in the bustling confusion, and asked God to deliver us.

In a few moments, a small truck screeched to a halt in front of us. The driver, a Thai who was apparently a farmer from nearby, motioned us into the back. "We need to get to Chanthaburi," we yelled excitedly as we hopped onto the truck bed.

"I know, I know," he interrupted, speeding off in the direction of the city. Choked by the thick dust stirred up along the rugged road, we were unable to say another word. The driver, too, was silent for the entire thirty miles, until we pulled up in front of our hotel.

"Good-bye," he said as we got out, bare seconds before he drove away. Staring open-mouthed at the retreating truck, we wondered who he was or where he came from, an appearance still a mystery to us.

That same day, I learned later, a woman in California had stood up in her home church and said, "I believe God is telling us to pray for Margaret. I think she is in some kind of trouble." It was the obedience of these Christians, 8,000 miles away, that brought us out of our peril, safely back to the hotel.

Knowing God had called me to the camps of Thailand, I was confident of His protection. Once alarmed by the fearful stories coming out of Southeast Asia, I was soon comforted when the Lord gave me a Bible verse: "Behold, I send an Angel before thee, to keep thee in the way, and to bring thee into the place which I have prepared" (Exodus 23:20).

Right then I made up my mind never to be afraid again. Whatever God has in store for me, that is exactly what I want. If it includes dying for His work, I can't think of anything more precious.

God at Work in the Camps

A year later the Lord brought me to the Vietnamese camp at Laem Sing. It is inhabited by a thousand refugees, of whom more than three hundred are Christians. Warmed by the fresh breeze blowing from the Gulf of Thailand, I sat on the hard floor of a split-bamboo house, eating rice and fish from a pressed wood table and listening to stories of courage and piracy as people described their ordeal of escape by sea from Communist Vietnam.

Mr. Chueng, for example, told of his voyage to freedom in a boat so tightly packed with refugees that each person had to sit up the whole time, knees pressed to knees. During the trip, the supplies of food, water, and fuel were exhausted. The people were forced to row the heavy wooden boat four days before reaching safety.

The minority who escape Communist gunfire and are not drowned at sea must face the attacks of pirating bandits, then hopelessness in a refugee camp, perhaps for the rest of their lives. The Christians feel this deprivation as strongly as anyone else, but the love of Jesus in their hearts gives them a markedly different outlook.

On the day a former Communist informer arrived on one of the refugee boats, many in the camp were ready to kill him immediately.

"No, don't kill him," pleaded the Christians.

"Turn him over to us, instead."

Reluctantly, the camp leaders put this despised adversary into the hands of the Christians. Though hating what he had done, they loved the man as a child of God, and he was soon won to Christ. Repenting of his former evil, he now serves a new Master.

Before my stay at Laem Sing, the Christians had decided they should build a church for the camp. Selecting a large, flat area on which to build, the group secured permission from the Chinese woman who owned a family grave site nearby and began hauling huge rocks from the beach, to form a foundation.

"You must stop!" the Chinese woman suddenly ordered, after construction was well underway. "Too close to grave."

Surprised and upset, the Christians tried to reason with her, until it became apparent she wanted a bribe.

"I'm sorry, we don't pay bribes," they told her and meekly moved to another, more difficult site. Before leaving, however, they cleaned up the area and put flowers on the grave, to show their love for the woman despite her faithlessness.

At the new location, the people were forced to break up large boulders, with only two pickaxes, and hammer each rock into gravel for a foundation. When this backbreaking work was completed, a cement floor could be poured. In a gesture of Christian brotherhood, the Cambodian refugees at the Gom Put camp sent small tree trunks to be used for lumber, and the church slowly took shape.

Dedication day was one of pride and gratitude, as the congregation sat on a floor covered with a black plastic tarp and sang praises to the Lord. Today, the church stands proudly on the Gulf, an outpost of God in a sad and lonely exile.

I worked at the Trat camp, riding with missionary Don Cobb daily, staying alone in a Thai hotel at Chanthaburi, and traveling through the most dangerous part of the border region. I was the only Caucasian staying in the Thai hotel. Giving the impression of poverty, as I had been advised—take off rings, wear old clothes, don't even take a suitcase—I slept in a dingy room on the hardest bed I have ever lain on, watching a slowly circulating fan in the ceiling stir the stale air. No one was there to protect me—no one spoke English—but the Lord watched over me the whole time, and that is the best protection I know.

On my first morning there I went to the restaurant across the street for breakfast. As in the hotel, no one knew English. As best I could, I ordered orange juice, coffee, and toast, and then the fun began.

The waiter poured orange soda pop from a bottle into a glass of ice cubes and gave it to me for orange juice. Instead of coffee, I was brought a cup of hot tea. Gesturing frantically, I tried to describe that I wanted coffee. In response, the waiter brought half a cup of coffee with a cup of sweetened evaporated milk to go with it—Thai style. I needed something to dilute the strong coffee so, pointing to the milk, I shook my head and repeated "water, water." The obliging waiter returned with another glass of ice cubes, into which he poured cold water.

"Hot, hot," I said, fanning my brow in an attempt to convey the idea that I wanted hot water. At last, he brought the hot water, and we both smiled happily.

There I sat, surrounded by cups and glasses of liquid—six in all. The other patrons watched with interest to see what this crazy *fahrong* (foreigner) was going to do with all those drinks. Turning around, I saw quite an audience gathered behind me, watching in amazement. Seeing the humor of the situation, I obliged them by sipping from each container consecutively, then turned and smiled at my fans. Caught between amusement and consternation, they realized I was putting on a show for them, and we all laughed hilariously.

At the Trat camp, I helped teach a Bible lesson and saw many people turn to God. One of the refugees, who had lost his mind because of the incredible carnage he had witnessed in Cambodia, was lashed to a post with heavy chains, where he raved almost constantly, a terrible witness to the atrocities back home.

Moved by compassion, the missionaries and I laid hands on the man and prayed for his healing. Soon, he quieted down enough that he could be unchained and attend our Christian meetings. But the greatest triumph came after we left, when he was completely healed through prayer by the Christians in the camp. How their faith grew when they realized that God would use them—not just foreign missionaries—to do such a mighty work!

The Lord's protection continued as we left the Trat camp, narrowly escaping a Communist mortar attack on the road back to town. More than fifteen people were killed in that barrage, but we were spared by passing the area just before it began. God had more work scheduled for us in the camps of Thailand.

Never Too Old!

Committed to answering the Lord's call sending me to the refugees, I was bewildered when, on my arrival in Bangkok, I had been rejected for service by the two religious organizations to which I had been sent.

"You're too old," they said. "I'm afraid we can't

use you. What could *you* do?"

Since the Thais are very restrictive in letting people into the camps, missionary organizations reflect this reluctance, for fear of losing their own access. These organizations donate more than three million dollars a year in food, clothing, medicine, housing, and other necessities. Without this supplement to the steadily decreasing UN aid, the refugees would starve.

After ten days of unsuccessful attempts to secure an entry pass, I fell on my knees. "What did You bring me here for?" I asked the Lord woefully. "I can't get into a single camp."

I'm more interested in you *than any work you can do.* The Lord's answer came as a distinct inward impression. *Your faith and patience have been growing. When it is time for you to go, you will go. I will open the doors that others have shut.*

In a Sunday church service not long afterward, I was surprised to spot a gray-haired lady sitting in the congregation. In an area staffed mostly by young missionaries, it is quite unusual to see an older person.

"I'm Mrs. Callaway," the woman responded cheerfully, after I introduced myself. "My husband and I are serving under World Vision at the Chingkam camp."

We spent the rest of day together, becoming acquainted and sharing stories of God's work. Finally she said, "Would you like to visit us at the camp?"

Would I? She was just about the only person in Bangkok who could get me into one! I praised the Lord for coming through again.

We visited the camp and held services with the forty Christians there, taking communion of weak tea and a pinch of boiled rice. The faith of these people is a miracle itself. Outnumbered overwhelmingly by animist worshipers who maintain just a thin shell of Buddhism over their ancient religion, Christians must make a personal sacrifice to accept Jesus Christ. All their idols, fetishes, and often-valuable antiquities must be burned publicly, to prove a real commitment to the Lord.

After working at Chingkam for a while, I found an assignment with Alice Compain at the Bangkok transit center. Here, refugees stay after leaving the camps, waiting for a sponsor to bring them to France, Australia, or the United States. Alice taught French to the first group, and I taught English to the rest, using the Bible as our textbook. Many accepted the Lord as they realized for the first time that God is not a stone idol, but a living Person.

Later, I was allowed to teach English to fifty Vietnamese children at Din Dang, another transit center in Bangkok. While students in most classrooms sit in rows, mine were in layers, because we were crowded into a small storeroom, sitting on stacks of boxes arranged in stair-step fashion. Nearly seven hundred Vietnamese live in this two-story concrete building, awaiting transit to a new life, and it was my privilege to teach the children something about the love of Jesus.

"He was a refugee, too," I told them, sparking their interest in a God who could understand how they felt.

Although I encountered constant problems in renewing my visa, which is good for only thirty days at a time in Thailand, the Lord kept me there for six months in His service. The refugees could not get over the fact that a woman of my age would come all the way from America, just to share the love of Jesus with them.

From Prison to Praise

In Bangkok, a beautiful, dark-haired young English girl named Rita Nightengale sits in a jail cell, faced with a twenty-year sentence for smuggling heroin. Her case has received much notoriety because of the very unusual circumstances. I visited Rita every week, and we became good friends—as close as one can become when talking through double-barred doors.

Rita had traveled the world for adventure, but when she became engaged to a wealthy Chinese

man, her fling came to an end. Sending her with a
friend to Bangkok to prepare for their wedding,
her fiance failed to come as promised. Instead,
she was arrested at the airport, with a suitcase full
of drugs, and soon convicted of smuggling—an
extremely serious crime.

"I was used as a drug runner," Rita complained
bitterly. Thrown into a cell with eight Thai
women and sitting on the hard floor to eat meager
rice meals and sleep, she resented everyone who
came near and hated the world which had treated
her so cruelly.

I talked to Rita about Jesus. As the visits continued, her heart began to melt. "I feel a love in
your heart toward me," she said wonderingly.
"Why would you love me?"

"That is the love Jesus has planted in me," I
answered gently, "and it is being projected
through me to you. God loves you, too."

A Christian friend and I gave a Bible and some
Christian books to Rita, and one day we noticed a
marked change in her. Gone was the bitterness
over the injustice of her confinement. For the first
time, her face reflected perfect peace, for she had
accepted Jesus as her Saviour.

"Since I have Christ, I'm happy," she beamed.
"I know He let me come here for a reason." The
guards were amazed at the change, as she finally
accepted her situation. Refusing to plead guilty
to receive a reduced sentence, Rita is steadfastly

trusting the Lord for His will for her future.

As I said my farewell, she prayed aloud for the first time.

"Jesus, thank You for Mrs. Cole. Please take care of her as she returns home." Such a simple prayer, but full of meaning for both of us. That prayer has become one of my earthly treasures.

When Every Penny Counted

One of the most exciting experiences I had was at the Chingkam camp. The Christians there had been holding meetings in the tiny longhouse cubicles with no privacy. "Wouldn't it be wonderful if we had a meeting place in which we could worship?" they often dreamed.

Hearing of this need, I was struck by a sudden thought. Before I left California for Thailand, Calvary Church in Torrance, pastored by the Reverend Wilbur Wacker, had presented me with an offering of $514.30. Perhaps I could give some of it to these people.

"How much money would you need?" I asked.

"About three hundred dollars," they responded, after carefully figuring it out. I gave the money quietly and cheerfully.

Soon a little meeting place was built, with a dirt floor, woven bamboo for sides, and a tin roof. They were so proud of this little building—the only thing in the world they could call their own.

A three-day celebration was held in dedication. The first day, they devoted to praising God; on the second, a love feast was given for the whole camp; the final day, they held the first service in the new structure, happily baptizing eighteen new Christians. In their enthusiasm for God, they have increased the Christian population of that camp in a few months from forty to two hundred, and it is still growing rapidly.

But the story does not end there.

As I was preparing to return home several months later, I received a letter from the Gom Put camp, near Chanthaburi, where I had walked in unnoticed by the guards. In reply to my question about their need for a meeting place, they wrote: "We have heard about your donation to the Chingkam camp, and we pray you will help build a Christian meeting place for our camp, too."

Enclosed was a detailed diagram of their proposed building and a price list for everything needed to build it, down to the last nail. The needed sum was $214.30, the exact balance of the offering from home!

Not needing the money, I had felt embarrassed for accepting the church's offering. Now, I was humbly astonished at God's marvelous planning for the needs of His people in this impoverished land. I could hardly refuse to give the money, when God's hand was so obviously in it. Once

again, all the arrangements were left to Him, and
that has proven to be the best arrangement of all.
But soon, I would find that leaving everything to
God is not always easy—especially when facing
prison.

5
At the Ends of the Earth

As our plane made its bumpy descent into the sweltering heat of Rangoon, capital of Burma, my palms were moist with excitement. *Here I am, joining the ranks of the big-time Bible smugglers,* I smiled to myself.

All the arrangements had been made to bring me through the tough customs inspection, and the fact the plane was three hours late—after being repaired for a "slight collision," I had been told—was only slight cause for concern.

Or was it?

My contact in immigration was to pass me through without difficulty, but what if he had given up waiting for the plane?

"Whatever you do," I had been emphatically warned, "don't take in more than two Bibles. If they catch you with that, you'll only be deported. With more than two, they can throw you into jail as a wholesaler."

I was bringing in eight! Without my friend in customs, I could not successfully smuggle the Bibles in, since they were in plain sight in my suitcase.

Earlier, I had tried to help God out by disguising them. "I'll just put some other book covers on the Bibles," I had mused. "They'll think I'm an avid reader." Yet when I finished covering the Bibles, an inward voice said, *That's not the way I want it done.*

"Okay, Lord," I sighed, obediently removing the false covers. I stared apprehensively at the large words in Burmese on the front of each book—*The Holy Bible.*

"This will never do," I muttered, and began taking the pebbled black covers off each Bible in another feeble attempt at disguise. Again the voice: *Are you ashamed of My Word?*

"Oh, no, Lord," I replied quickly, "but we have to get them in somehow."

You're not going to smuggle those Bibles in, came the response. *You're going to carry them in!*

"All right, Lord," I said in resignation, packing them right on top in my suitcase. If there is one thing I have learned in my travels, it is to obey God's voice when I hear it, no matter what I may think about the plan.

While in Malaysia only a few days before, I had met two people just returned from Burma, who told me of the great need for Bibles and other materials. In response, I collected some Gospel records and books in Burmese, along with the Bibles, and was ready to aid those beleaguered Christians.

Now, as we left the plane and headed toward customs, my confidence was not quite so high. "It's just You and me," I said shakingly.

Do you need anybody else? came the inward reply.

"Of course not," I grinned, with a sudden surge of inner assurance.

But arriving at customs, I was horrified to discover that the shift had changed and my contact was long gone. And if that were not enough, Matthew Win—the man from Campus Crusade for Christ who was supposed to meet me at the door and bring me out—was not there, either. With no earthly hand to guide me, I walked alone to the customs table.

Entering a tightly controlled country is not the same as visiting a tourist mecca. Each visitor is carefully checked for cameras, books, and other valuables. This is followed by a thorough luggage search and a declaration of the exact amount of money carried. Upon leaving, any difference in the audits must be accounted for.

This day, the customs men were being especially thorough, frisking people in line ahead of me. "O Lord," I whispered, "save me!"

My turn came, and my heavy luggage—loaded with books—was heaved onto the table with a thump. Trying valiantly to smile, I waited as the customs agent looked sternly into my face. Considering for a moment what to do, his hard face suddenly softened.

"We don't open older mothers' luggage," he grinned. "Just go on through."

Shoulders sagging with relief, I walked out of the customs area and started crying. The Lord was all I had, and He was all I needed.

It wasn't long before He solved the problem of distributing the Bibles to the right people, as well. Soon after I checked into my hotel room, the bellboy brought me some hot water. I watched his eyes grow big when he saw the Bibles.

"Are those Burmese Bibles?" he gasped in disbelief. "Could I buy one?"

"I'm sorry, they're not for sale," I responded, scrutinizing his face for a motive. Bibles are a valuable commodity in Burma. "Why do you want one?"

"I teach about a hundred people in our church," he explained eagerly, "and only one of us has a Burmese Bible. We have to write everything out, and I've been praying so long for a Bible to use."

"Well, I can't sell you one. But I can *give* you one," I smiled brightly, handing him one of the prized books. Overwhelmed with joy, we both cried like babies. I don't know who was happier: he for receiving a Bible, or I for giving it.

A desk clerk, a policewoman . . . all the Bibles found exactly the hands God intended. Then

Matthew Win, who had missed me at the airport because he was sent the wrong arrival date in a telegram, finally caught up with me.

"Your first speaking engagement is in an hour," he said breathlessly. "Many students from the Rangoon Institute of Technology are coming over to our building to hear you."

"Speaking engagement?" I repeated in astonishment. "But I'm not prepared to speak."

"Time to go," he answered. I spoke at that meeting and the following day, Sunday, addressed three large churches, totalling more than a thousand persons. My heart went out to these people, so in love with Jesus and so in need of Christian literature. In one church of five hundred, for example, no more than a dozen Bibles were available.

Burmese Christians are desperately hungry for word from their fellow believers in the outside world. Foreign missionaries were expelled from Burma in the mid-sixties, and visitors are limited to a one-week stay. With people poor and conditions primitive, the society is like a windup clock that is in the last stages of running down. Because few foreign goods are allowed into the country, repairs are makeshift. Streets and buildings are decaying; cars are incredibly old, and their lights are dimmed to conserve scarce batteries. A hospital patient must go to the black market for medicine.

Still, churches continue with quiet joy, courage, and resourcefulness in the homeland of the world's purest and strongest Buddhism. Christian demoninations grow in numbers and independence.

Matthew Win had my week planned out. "We sent announcements to fourteen churches, telling of a wonderful Bible teacher coming," he told me.

"Oh, who's that?" I asked.

"You, of course."

"*Me*? All I have are a few Bible outlines!"

"Time to go," came the calm reply once again. Every night that week I taught a group drawn from those churches, and my meager lessons were deeply appreciated. It is a thrill to be right where the need is greatest, for then God does the work, no matter what the person's qualifications.

During this period, I visited Sri Lanka, an even poorer island country off the tip of India, as a Youth for Christ speaker.

At a Christian orphanage at Kandy, I saw firsthand the difference that just a little care can make in the lives of these wretchedly poor children, many of whom live on the street, eating whatever they can find there. Accepting no money from the government, the orphanage operates purely on faith.

Shortly before my arrival, the orphanage's only cow was killed by a poisonous snake, and no milk was available for the forty-one children. I was able to buy them another cow with money entrusted to me by churches back home.

Introducing me to one of the church groups later, the orphanage head declared, "We had prayed that the Lord would send us another cow, and along came Mrs. Cole!"

The most difficult experience of my month in Sri Lanka was in a small town outside the capital of Colombo. I was met by a Christian, who invited me to stay in his home. "How generous," I thought to myself as I accepted his kind invitation.

Walking into the house, I was horrified to see great patches of green mold hanging from the ceiling. Being shut up all the time, the house overpowered me with its decaying smell. I was led to my ice-cold room, where I slept in my clothes against the wet blankets on the bed. Nothing worked in the bathroom, and one look in the kitchen was almost enough to give me food poisoning by osmosis.

It was late, so I had to spend a sleepless night in the house. The next morning, I was ready to leave.

"You don't have heat in the rooms, do you?" I asked my host, a dentist.

"Oh no, we never need heat," he replied graciously.

"I was very cold last night. Perhaps I had better move to the hotel," I returned.

"The hotel is terribly expensive, Mrs. Cole. I couldn't have you do that."

"Well, how much is it?" I asked.

"Five dollars a day," he announced, reluctant to reveal such a staggering figure.

"Well, maybe I should stay there for a couple of days," I replied, barely containing my joy at getting out of there.

At the hotel, though, my hopes were dashed. "No, we don't have heat, either," said the desk clerk. Suddenly, my thoughts flashed back to my prayer that God would allow me in some way to share the suffering of His loyal people. What was a little mold anyway?

I returned with the dentist to his home and determined to stay there. Then the most amazing thing happened. On my arrival, my eye had been swollen shut, blood red with painful infection. But after spending a second night at this house, I noticed that the infection was gone without a trace. Once again, the Lord had been testing my commitment, and I had passed—but barely!

6

A Fellowship of Suffering

With less than an hour before my tour group would leave for the airport, there I was, alone and lost in the middle of Moscow.

The heavy snowfall obscured my vision as I stumbled down the busy street, slipping repeatedly on the rapidly piling snowdrifts. At age seventy-one, it is easy to fall and break an ankle, especially when you are in a desperate hurry.

"Lord, please stop that cab!" I prayed aloud and waved frantically at an already-occupied taxi speeding by in the wrong direction. If only I could catch him, and if he drove quickly, I would reach the hotel in time. To my amazed delight, the taxi crunched to a stop in the snow.

"Thank You, Father," I cried, dashing to the waiting cab. Flashing the driver a slip of paper with the name of the hotel, I jumped in. From his tone I realized his bewildered resentment. We drove off at a leisurely pace to the other passenger's destination, then began a slow, winding trip to my hotel.

I glanced at my watch in impatient agitation. Only a miracle could bring me back in time. Since I had slipped away unnoticed from the darkened movie theater of the Lenin Museum, my tour guide would have no idea where to find me. Alone in a heavy blizzard, I imagined being stranded in Soviet Russia without the slightest excuse for my departure from the authorized tour.

Not particularly interested in the sights of Russia, this wasn't the first time I had left the tour. I was here for another purpose: to meet with beleaguered Russian Christians and present them a set of fifty New Testaments in their language.

On My Own

"You're too old," I had been told when volunteering to work with one of the organizations which regularly carries Bibles into the Soviet Union. Thrown at me in countries around the world, those three words always increased my determination; so I came to Russia on my own.

For several months I had felt a divine calling to carry Bibles into the USSR. First visiting several travel agencies at home in Southern California, I was told no tours were available and that arranging the necessary visa and group placement would take two or three months.

Taking my set of tiny New Testaments, I
boarded a plane for Europe. I was on my way to
Sri Lanka (Ceylon) and then to Thailand, where I
would work again with the refugees. Since I was
routed through Europe, I assumed that if God
wanted me to visit Russia, He would arrange it.
Otherwise, I'd leave the Bibles in Amsterdam
with an organization that could get them in.

Arriving in Europe, I visited a London tour
agency and then the Soviet consulate in Switzer-
land, but to no avail. Beginning to feel doubtful
about the chances of entering Russia, I flew to
Frankfurt for one last attempt.

Deplaning at the Frankfurt airport, I asked at
an information booth whether a travel agency
was nearby. "Look behind you," came the terse
reply. Turning, I spotted the agency less than ten
feet away, and walked over to it.

"Do you have any tours of Russia?" I asked.

"As a matter of fact, we have one leaving in
eight days," the agent replied. Having been arranged three months before by an agency in
Munich, the tour still had *one* opening. I knew
immediately that God had kept His finger on that
reservation, waiting just for me.

"I'll take it," I said quickly.

"You'd be out of your mind to go," she ob-
jected. "Everything will be in German. The
people on the tour all speak German, and the
Russian guides will lecture in that language. You

won't understand a word and won't know a thing about what you are being shown."

"That's all right," I smiled. "I'll go anyway."

Looking condescendingly at this crazy American, the agent explained that it would take considerable time to secure a visa. Counting the weekend and a coming holiday, there would be only four days to mail my passport to Bonn, have the visa processed, and return it by mail before the day of departure. To advance the paperwork in such a short time was absolutely impossible.

Then came the final blow. "You must pay now in full for the trip," the agent sighed with resignation. "If the visa does not arrive in time, there will be no refund. You will have lost your money."

At that point my Scotch blood rose to the surface. *Don't you dare waste money on such a gamble,* my mind insisted.

Immediately, however, another inner voice interrupted. *Trust God,* it seemed to say. There was a time when I would have immediately obeyed my first impulse, but God has taught me many things over the years, foremost among them being to trust His promises. Pulling out my traveler's checks, I paid the full fare.

Now with eight days of unexpected leisure in a foreign land, I wondered where to stay. I had heard of a place called Canaan Land, in Darmstadt, which was not too far away, and decided to see about a room.

Arriving at this retreat of the Evangelical Lutheran Sisters, I rang the bell on the heavy iron gate. One of the sisters greeted me warmly and asked in heavily accented German if I was Mrs. Coke. Supposing that she meant "Cole," I said yes, and she invited me in.

I was escorted to a lovely room, and the nearby bathroom had a luxurious tub. I was going to enjoy my eight-day rest!

But about the same time that I began to wonder how they knew I was coming, they began wondering where my husband and children were. They really had been expecting the Coke family!

Questioning who I was and where I was going, they were delighted when I said I was on my way to Thailand. That was the magic word, for a group of sisters had adopted that country as their special prayer project.

After I told them about my work in Thailand, they found a small room for me, even though they couldn't really spare it, and took me to their hearts. I spent a delightful week there, walking garden pathways and talking to other missionaries from many countries.

Two days before the scheduled departure of my tour, I hesitantly placed a call to the travel agency.

"Your visa is here!" the voice on the phone exclaimed in disbelief. "They processed it in one day. We have never heard of such a thing!" But God had assured me that is exactly what would happen.

Early Saturday morning I arrived at the airport, ready for my divinely planned trip to Russia. The handsome young tour guide, who spoke English, looked at me blankly when I informed him that I was part of his group.

"You're not on my tour," he frowned. "I arranged it three months ago in Munich, so I should know. We have eighty-nine reservations and no cancellations."

He remained unconvinced when I showed him my ticket, and I was forced to go downstairs and bring the ticket agent to prove I had a reservation.

Bewildered, the tour guide counted the people and checked them against his list. Everyone was present, yet each time he counted, there were exactly eighty-nine of us—including me. "This is very peculiar," he muttered to himself as we boarded the plane for Russia. He was to shake his head and repeat the same phrase many times on the tour. He just couldn't understand God's arithmetic!

Meeting With the Underground

On our second day in Moscow, my excitement grew as our group went sightseeing in the area where my Christian contacts lived. I wondered how God was ever going to get me away from the tour group, but He had it all arranged.

An English-speaking tour group came up directly behind us, and I saw my chance. "This lecture is much too interesting to miss!" I exclaimed to my guide. "Would you mind if I joined the other group, so I can understand it?"

Reluctantly, he agreed and explained how to take a taxi back to the hotel if I became separated from the group. And wouldn't you know, I was separated right away! Jumping into a cab, I showed the address of my contact to the driver.

Moments later we stopped before a huge complex of apartment buildings. Gazing at the forbidding, multistoried concrete structures, grounds overgrown with weeds, I felt my confidence sag.

"How will I ever find my contact here?" I moaned to myself. Hundreds of families must be housed here, spread over a huge area. Since I spoke no Russian, the chances of finding the right one were slim.

But God had taken care of that, too. As I stood surveying the complex in bewilderment, a young woman with a beautiful smile approached. I stepped up to her, in the faint hope she might understand enough to help me.

"Why, that's me!" she exclaimed in Russian when I showed her the address on a slip of paper.

I couldn't believe my ears!

Isn't that just like the Lord, to have me bump into the right person?

Entering the narrow living room of her tiny apartment, I was immediately struck by the sight of a large pencil drawing of Jesus dominating one wall. This gave me an instant clue to the caliber of the Christians in Russia—beaten down but not broken, unashamed of their faith in a living Saviour.

With the help of a small phrase book and a Russian-English dictionary, we were able to communicate quite well amid exaggerated gestures and curious facial expressions. "I'm Mrs. Cole, from America," I said hopefully. But she wasn't expecting me. When I produced the fifty New Testaments hidden in my clothing and my shoulder bag, the change was electric.

"Oh!" she gasped. "So many!" A grin of delight spread across her face, and I knew the Bibles would be put to good use. Her excitement continued as I shared letters from Christian friends in America.

A Fugitive for Faith

True Christian sisters now, we talked of the Lord and His love. She recounted the beatings Christians had received from the secret police and the fugitive life of her sick husband, who was forced to hide with friends and leave her alone with their children. My cheeks hot with tears, I learned how he is denied work because of his faith. Their children are mocked and tormented by teachers and fellow students alike; even the small ones are interrogated by the police about their father's secret visits home.

The KGB had entered the apartment on many occasions and beaten her husband without mercy as she looked on helplessly. Sometimes she, too, was thrown around, but they suffered in silence.

"KGB?" I asked with a punching motion, referring to the secret police. She shook her head and folded her hands in prayer. "KGB," she replied firmly. She didn't hate those cruel men; she prayed for them!

Kissing my tears away, she pointed to the word *privilege* in the dictionary, never losing the radiant smile from her face. "*Radi Crista,*" she said joyfully, indicating the picture of Jesus. "For the sake of Christ." My own faith leaped when I realized it was a privilege for her to suffer for Jesus.

Leaving reluctantly for school, her ten-year-old daughter pointed to me and asked, "*Radi Crista?*" Did I also suffer for Jesus? I cannot remember any time I felt so utterly worthless, so insignificant.

Those of us in freedom hardly know what suffering is, although we may call our small problems by that name. The Russian Christians feel the dull agony of persecution every day, year after year. To ease their pain, all they need do is renounce their fatih. But that is the one thing they will not do.

Knowing that the print in the Testaments I brought was extremely small, I determined to leave money for the purchase of plastic magnifying glasses. Because it was dangerous for her to accompany me while I exchanged my traveler's checks for rubles, I agreed to return the following day with the money.

That day, my tour guide authorized me to walk the mile to the only bank in Moscow that will exchange foreign currency. Passing the long lines of women waiting outside poorly stocked stores and fighting over such delicacies as overripe grapes and wilted cabbages, I arrived at the bank and stood in line to cash my check. Later, spending two more hours conversing with my friend in her apartment, I learned that her friends had meanwhile taken those little Bibles with trembling hands and tearfully prayed that God would make them worthy to have His Word. I felt deeply grateful that the Lord had allowed me to bring them.

Lost and Found

By now I sensed it was time to leave, realizing I should not try to contact anyone else, for fear of jeopardizing them. With a growing uneasiness about being followed, I said good-bye and headed for the subway, instead of the usual taxi. That was a big mistake.

Descending the fast-moving escalator into the cavernous subway tunnel, I hardly noticed the glistening chandeliers and the beautiful artwork which make the Moscow subway so famous. I hurriedly selected a train that seemed to be headed in the right direction and rode until it felt as if we had traveled all the way to the border, five hundred miles away.

Convinced of my mistake, I jumped off the train at the next stop and showed the paper containing the name of my hotel to several people. Receiving only scowls and grunts of disinterest in return, I felt frantic and prayed, "Lord, save me!"

Through the crowd I spotted three teenage girls wearing ballet stockings. One of the girls was smiling at me. That was all I needed! I rushed over and asked if they knew my hotel. To my astonishment, the smiling one spoke perfect English!

"We'll be happy to take you there," she said brightly. "Just let me ask directions." Talking to several people, she finally found a man who knew the hotel and received instructions for reaching it.

The girls escorted me onto one of the trains and brought us through the maze of interconnections back to my hotel. Shuddering with relief once it was over, I thanked them and offered return train fare, but they refused it. God sent them to me just when I was so desperate. Sometimes I feel my guardian angel must work overtime to rescue me from these situations.

Since the hotel lobby was crowded with another tour, I entered unnoticed. The woman who monitors the coming and going of each guest on my floor was missing from her station, so I returned to my room without having to explain my absence. I spent the evening in prayers of thanks, including a sermon about Jesus' love and salvation for the eavesdroppers listening through hidden microphones. (My contact in America had warned that the rooms were bugged, for he had helped do it before escaping from Russia.)

A Farewell Offering

Just before I fell asleep, glad this was my last night in Russia, God put a definite impression on my heart for one more mission: to cash another one-hundred-dollar check and give it to the family I had been visiting. "I'll do it, Lord," I agreed immediately, leaving details to Him.

Sneaking away from the Lenin Museum tour the next morning, I trudged through the freezing gale and blinding snow to the bank where I could cash my check. With only an hour or two before our group left for the airport, time was critical.

Without the usual long line at the bank, I could make it.

On my arrival at the bank, I was horrified to see it completely empty. "They're closed," I thought, remembering the preparations under way for the October Revolution celebration. What a relief! The tellers were there. Walking up to one, I presented my check. In no time, it was cashed, my visa stamped, and I was out into a waiting taxi.

Reaching my friend's apartment for the last time, I kissed her surprised face, put the money in her hand, and waved good-bye. Had I been able to, I would have given her every cent I had, but there would be enough trouble at customs as it was explaining where my money went.

The warm memory of my friend faded as I suddenly jerked back into the present. Still staring at my watch, I realized how the minutes had slipped away. The taxi driver was taking his time driving to the hotel, even stopping at a kiosk for cigarettes and some conversation. My departure time crept steadily closer. "Lord, You have to help me again," I pleaded as we took the longest possible route.

When at last we arrived, my heart sank. The bus was gone. "Maybe they're still at the restaurant," I muttered hopefully. Racing up to my room, I threw my clothes into the suitcases and walked the six blocks to the restaurant as fast as I could, heedless of the stinging snowfall.

Once again the Lord plucked me out of disaster. Our tour group was still eating. I strolled in, trying to look nonchalant, nodded self-assuredly to the tour guide, and collapsed into a chair. My mission accomplished, I slumped in exhaustion, to eat still another Russian cabbage meal. There is no mistaking when the cabbage crop is in!

Confrontation at the Airport

It was midafternoon when we arrived at the Moscow airport. All of us were anxious to hurry through customs and leave for home. One by one, our tour members passed the inspector, leaving me nearly the last to go through. Stepping up for my turn, I was stopped cold.

"Give me the key to your suitcase," barked the burly Russian official. As I handed it over, another inspector grabbed my purse and swung my flight bag down off my shoulder. Realizing they must have something on me, my nerves buckled. Had the unauthorized excursions been noticed? Did they think I was a spy?

I felt queasy as the inspectors pawed through my luggage, closely examining every scrap of paper and carefully pressing their fingers along the hem of every article of clothing. Two strings of costume-jewelry beads were broken and scattered in a search for smuggled gold. My book of

Russian phrases was meticulously examined for possible secret codes. I was glad that my Russian contact had refused to write letters for me to deliver to Christians back home! She knew better than I what kind of a government we were dealing with.

"What is this?" the inspector growled, holding a rock I had picked up outside the Pushkin Palace for my daughter. A vision of the infamous Soviet mental institutions flashed into my mind. Were they testing me to see whether I belonged there?

"That is a rock," I replied firmly.

"It is against the law to take even a stone from this country. Why are you taking it? To analyze the mineral content?" the official snapped.

Knowing it sounded terribly foolish, I told the truth. "It's for my daughter's rock collection."

With a sneer, he kept the rock and held up the next exhibit, my pocket camera. "Where is the microfilm?" he demanded.

"That's just a tourist camera," I insisted shakily. "Here, you can have all the film, if you want it!" They did confiscate the film but eventually returned the camera.

After they inspected every item, I was ordered to follow a heavy woman in uniform to a cubicle, where I was told to take off my clothes. These, too, were closely examined. After dressing, I was brought to a nasty-looking little man for interrogation.

Looking through me with piercing gray eyes, the man asked question after question: Why had I come to Russia? Who was I working for? Why was I the only American on a German tour? Where was the microfilm hidden?

"You are lying!" the man stormed as I tried my best to answer him without endangering my Christian friends.

More than praying for myself, I asked that God would protect the Christians who had received the Bibles, not wanting to put them in more danger than they already were. Thinking back on my excursions away from the tour, I now recalled seeing a rather pleasant-looking man around our hotel on several occasions. He had once approached me and asked how I liked Russia. And on my last return to the hotel, the taxi driver had come into the lobby and talked with two men. *Had they followed me the whole time? Did they know everything?*

By now I was deeply frightened. Before I had left them, the tour group had passed to the boarding area, and the plane was due for departure at any moment. For all I knew, it may have already left, stranding me here without a friend. Maybe the officials planned to charge me with staying in the country illegally!

A cold shudder raced through my body as the cruel little man ordered another search of my luggage. Thumbing through my remaining traveler's checks, he demanded to see everything

I had bought in the country. Waiting tensely for him to ask about the two missing one-hundred-dollar checks that I had cashed for my Russian friend, I realized there was no way I could explain where the money went without telling the whole story.

But God put a screen of protection around those checks and my visits to the apartment complex. Had I been questioned about them, I could never have answered.

A Peculiar Trip

After an hour and a half, the questioning abruptly ended, and I was told to go.

"Next time, tell the truth!" the man spat as I left the room. Running to the boarding area, I was greatly relieved that the plane was an hour and a half late. The tour group was still there. "Thank You, Lord," I cried, rejoining the group, weak from exhaustion.

"It is very peculiar," muttered our guide, shaking his head. He had found everything about my trip to Russia peculiar, but that is the way my Father in heaven likes to work.

Back in Frankfurt, I had found the only available spot on his tour. Since I knew no German, the guide thought it very strange that I would want to join a German-speaking group, but that was the only way I could enter Russia within a reasonable time. He was even more bewildered when a space miraculously appeared for me on the tour, which he was sure had been solidly booked, with no cancellations. Most unusual was my ability to obtain a visa in one day, a feat which the travel agent declared was absolutely impossible. But *impossible* is not a word in the heavenly vocabulary; a fact proven to me many times.

As we flew out of Russia into freedom, I praised the Lord for His protection and the privilege of meeting His mighty army in chains. Despite severe oppression, the church in Russia is growing. I learned that thirteen members of the elite Soviet Academy of Sciences have recently given up their positions for the sake of Christ. Christians are demonstrating openly to obtain their rights of worship as granted under the Soviet Constitution. As atheism reveals its emptiness to a new generation, many hundreds of new converts are baptized publicly every month. I have no doubt that God's people will ultimately prevail. ". . . If God be for us," the Bible asks, "who can be against us?" (Romans 8:31.)

Why would I, a senior citizen, risk ending my days in a Soviet prison to smuggle Bibles? This question was asked in Holland when I reported my experience to one of the Christian organizations based there.

"Don't you know that two Swedish boys spent more than six months in prison doing what you

did?" the director asked. "You should be home
with your grandchildren!"

"Well," I laughed, "this is hardly the first time
I've seen danger in the Lord's work. He's led me
all over the world." I smiled as I recounted the
exciting adventures God had brought me through
in Papua New Guinea, Guatemala, Thailand,
Burma, and now Russia. "I plan to keep going as
long as He wants me. I don't have too many years
ahead, you know, so I want each day to count."

7

A Lesson in Faith

Papua New Guinea. Guatemala. Thailand and Burma. Into the heart of Soviet Russia. Eyes gleam in every audience, as I tell the stories of what I experienced in God's service around the world.

Looking back, I am glad I didn't sit home and let my remaining years go to waste. Instead, I claimed God's Word as my promise: "As I was with Moses, so I will be with thee: I will not fail thee, nor forsake thee . . . . Be strong and of a good courage: be not afraid, neither be thou dismayed; for the Lord thy God is with thee withersoever thou goest" (*see* Joshua 1:5, 9).

In remote places I proved the truth of that promise, learning the lesson of faith one step at a time. I had heard about it, read of it in the Bible, and found inspiration by hearing accounts of others' faith. But the day I stepped out of my little boat of security—as Peter stepped out on the surface of the water at Jesus' invitation—was the time that I began to *experience* it.

My first step was not so difficult. Sent to New

113

Guinea by a Christian organization, I lived on a large base, where I was surrounded by fellow Christians and all of my needs were met. I prayed at that time that I might learn to know God better and place less value on material things. He answered my prayers and moved me up to the next stage.

The second lesson was my Guatemalan experience. Arriving without knowing where my path would lead, I was tested by God, to see if I could rely on Him to make the plans for me. Expecting to stay with Wycliffe, I had much to learn when God led me down a different path.

Thailand came as a challenge and an opportunity. Knowing no one, unsure of where I would stay or what I would do, I traveled there just because a need existed. The details had to be left to God.

My fourth step was into Burma, where there would be a little more danger. When my contacts failed to appear at customs, I was totally dependent on God to bring me through.

Finally, I entered Russia. I knew exactly where I was going, but also realized that it would be far more dangerous than any previous experience. By then my faith was stronger. Just as a baby learns to walk, I had been strengthened by practice and had discovered one important thing: to keep my eyes on Jesus alone.

As long as Peter did that, he was safe. But he

looked down, and a doubt formed as he saw the
raging waves beneath him. He had time only for a
quick prayer, the shortest in the Bible: "Lord,
save me!" Jesus' hands were already out-
stretched, ready to lift Peter up.

I felt the same way a few times, and He was
always there to help. Lost on a Russian subway,
alone on a street corner in Guatemala City,
ruthlessly interrogated by a Soviet official, I
could only turn to Jesus and cry silently for help.
Each time, He was ready to lift me out; not back
to a place of security and comfort, but to another
challenge of ever-increasing faith.

Was there a cost, a price to pay? Yes, indeed. I
could not deny that. My family, friends, doctor,
and a comfortable way of life were at home. I left
a car, comfortable bed, and the delicious food I
sometimes dreamed about. Pammy, my three-
year-old granddaughter, whom I longed to cud-
dle, was always in my thoughts, as were my older
grandchildren. They are very precious to me.

It's amazing how many things we take for
granted. I missed the worship services in my
church, where I had friends, gave and received
love in the congregation, and where I was able to
sit relaxed in a seat with a back and enjoy the
beautiful music of a choir.

I longed for the joy of a radio, over which I
could listen both to the news of my country and
to Christian programs, with their inspiration and

teaching. The holidays were a special time of
longing, for I knew family and friends would be
together back home, carving a turkey or picnick-
ing on a grassy park lawn.

Modern bathrooms, my little dog, Buffy, a pro-
fessional hairdresser—the list could go on in-
definitely. All these things had been an uncon-
scious part of my life for decades, and now I was
without them.

Was there anything left for me? Absolutely! I
still had the promise of Jesus, given to the disci-
ples when they left everything to follow Him:
". . . There is no man that hath left house, or
parents, or brethren, or wife, or children, for the
kingdom of God's sake, Who shall not receive
manifold more in this present time, and in the
world to come life everlasting" (Luke 18:29
italics mine). There was my promise. Jesus had
spelled it out.

Everlasting life would certainly be reward
enough, but what of the "manifold more" in this
present time? Among other things, I had virtually
perfect health during the times overseas, a real
blessing to a person my age. My one major illness
was completely healed by God, without the aid of
a doctor.

My style of eating changed, supplying the dis-
cipline I had always lacked. I lost a good deal of
weight and probably added years to my life. My
digestion improved noticeably.

Instead of the weekly routine of church services, I learned to worship in my own way. So many times I had mouthed the words, "I can do all things through Christ who strengtheneth me"; now I was *doing* some of those things and finding out I had capabilities unknown to me. I worshiped constantly, developing a new, close friendship with God, and spending hours alone reading, praying, and talking to Him.

Removed from the pressures and tensions we live under in America, I received the blessings of peace and a slower pace of life. No traffic problems existed to jangle my nerves; sometimes not even a telephone was present to disturb my reflections.

Exotic scenery filled my consciousness as I enjoyed the sight of rare birds and flowers, traveled to historic locations never seen by the average tourist, and found adventure among people strange to our culture.

One of the most important rewards of my days in far-off lands was the extended family God gave me to replace mine at home. In every place I found myself, God supplied lovely people to be part of my life. Those who are Christians always had stories to relate about what God had done for them. It seemed something like heaven will be: people from all parts of the world and all kinds of backgrounds, telling what God had done.

Especially important were the children who

flocked around me everywhere I went. I was "granny" to many of them, from refugee children to the sons and daughters of missionaries for whom I baby-sat.

I'll never forget the fifty or so children in the Bangkok refugee transit center and how they cried when I left them to return home. We had a nice party—tablecloths and cookies from the guest house where I lived, a cake made and decorated by a dear friend, balloons, party hats—and then it was time to say good-bye. Kissing each little girl and shaking hands with the little boys, I crossed the street to meet the bus.

Hurrying to the bus stop, I turned and noticed a little raggedy refugee army following me right down the middle of Din Dang road! As they caught up with me, I was surrounded by the wail of tearful children. My heart was almost broken as I stepped on the bus and was whisked away from these beautiful children of God, perhaps never to see them again in this life.

Looking back on the work God had led me to do, I began to see a pattern. He didn't send me to the leaders of the world; others have that mission. Instead, He brought me among the lowly, downtrodden people who were hurting the most. Standing among the refugees of the camps in Thailand—people who had left all they had, often including their families, many fleeing for their very lives with no promise whatever of a future where they might rebuild a new, permanent life—I seemed to feel the suffering in God's heart for these children of His, brutally displaced by the attacks of evil.

I cried for His beloved people in Russia, where cruel persecution continues day after day, for the Mam Indians in Guatemala, and His beloved family members in tribal New Guinea, along with those who never heard His name. I felt a closeness to the heart of Jesus as I shared their burdens and suffered with them.

But I am fortunate that I can return home to family and friends, to a free and wealthy country. Sadly, too many think only of themselves and what they can gain. I began to wonder: Is there a place for us who are retired—who have left our busy lives of material gain behind—to visit the unfortunates in far-off lands? I believe there is.

Those who have retired shouldn't think of this as the end of their useful lives. Why not *retread* and visit a field of mission?

So many people take sightseeing tours today. They shoot a few pictures of attractions on the tourist trails, send home some postcards, overeat in hotels, and think they've seen the country. Why not take a look at God's work, meet His family, offer some service, and watch the rewards?

The saddest part of old age is loneliness and the feeling of not being needed. I felt this when some of the missionary agencies turned me down because of my age. But God always finds a way. He wants older people, too. I have never been given great and wonderful things to do, but my Father finds little places for me to serve, all over the world. Perhaps I am not making an earth-shaking contribution, but I am happy and fulfilled, and perhaps I have made some small contribution to the kingdom of God.

Each time I return home, God opens doors for me to tell others of what is happening overseas. I have seen the needs, heard unusual stories, and witnessed divine miracles. Then I have been able to share my experiences with people back in America.

Since returning from my last trip two months ago, I have spoken seventeen times in churches and other meetings, becoming acquainted with many I never would have met otherwise. Some have given money, as God told them to, but it all goes directly to meet a need I have discovered in one of the places God has sent me. It is exciting to see how He always manages to exactly match a gift with a need.

But you don't have to travel to a far-off land to serve God. Plenty of worthwhile things can be found to do at home. Just ask for God's direction. Give your life in service for Him—no matter what your age—and watch Him open up opportunities directly suited to you. His divine employment agency has an infinite number of exciting openings, and He never misses in suiting the job exactly to the person.

Be assured that this book is not *my* story—it is *His* story. He planned and purposed it—and I followed His divine leading. All praise goes directly to Him!

Many have asked me, "Where to next?" My reply is always the same: "Wherever God leads me." My most exciting trip lies ahead, when some happy day He gives me the final call, and I will travel into outer space and beyond—home to Him. Until that time, I plan to keep going in His service, for I know that you're never too old for God.

Epilogue

After I returned home from my fourth missionary journey, I went to Far East Broadcasting Company in Whittier, California, where my Russian contact works. I discussed my trip into the Soviet Union with him.

He assured me that the Russian Christians knew I had gotten out of Russia safely. He told me of the apartment-house watchers who report the visit of a foreigner to any certain apartment. Undoubtedly I had been under surveillance, because three times I had visited the apartment of a family known to them as leading Christian dissidents.

While I was led to believe it was microfilm they were looking for, it was in all probability letters or information from the Christians being sent to sources in America. This is most offensive to the Russians, since they are anxious to create a good "human rights" image. The underground church knew of this danger and refused to write or send anything by me.

Two Swedish men, Sareld and Engstrom, were

searched as they were leaving Russia. Letters were found on them, and they were in prison at the time I was there. I was ignorant of that fact then, and might well have joined them had I not been protected.

In the home of my Russian contact friend in Whittier, I met his wife and family as well as his dear mother (who spent six years in a prison in Siberia for her faith). During this time her son was put into a state home and indoctrinated into atheism. It didn't take.

Later the State was about to take *his* children from him since he was a Christian and an unfit parent, when miraculously he was able to leave the country and now lives here. As I put my arms around these dear people, I felt I was indeed holding some of the Father's choice servants—tried and true—not found wanting—pure gold!

When I admire these wonderful Christians, I remember those still suffering in Russia. Then I think of my own Christian groups. Yes, we praise God for the good things He gives—but seldom do we hear praise for the suffering He allows and considers us worthy to bear. This was chief message I brought home from my Russian visit.

The Cracked Vessel

2 Timothy 2:20

In the Master's house many vessels stood
Some of wood, some silver and gold
And one there was made of clay of the Earth
It was cracked, uncomely and old.
But the vessel was purged, and hoped in its heart
That the Master would choose it someday—
Perhaps find a place where an old earthen vessel
Could be used in some very small way.
And there came a day when the kind Master said,
"I've a service just special for you,
Midst the lowly downtrodden, unlovely of Earth
Where a fine vessel would not do."
And into this cracked earthen vessel He placed
A great treasure—His love—deigned to go
To His needy. And out from the vessel it
    poured—
There was nothing to hinder its flow.

MARGARET RICE COLE

125

Other Marshall Pickering Paperbacks

THE TORN VEIL

Sister Gulshan and Thelma Sangster

Gulshan Fatima was brought up in a Muslim Sayed family according to the orthodox Islamic code of the Shias.

Suffering from a crippling paralysis she travelled to England in search of medical help. Although unsuccessful in medical terms, this trip marked the beginning of a spiritual awakening that led ultimately to her conversion to Christianity.

Gulshan and her father also travelled to Mecca in the hope that God would heal her, but that trip too was of no avail. However, Gulshan was not detered. She relentlessly pursued God and He faithfully answered her prayers. Her conversion, when it came, was dramatic and brought with a miraculous healing.

The Torn Veil is Sister Gulshan's thrilling testimony to the power of God which can break through every barrier.

RELEASE
The Miracle of the Siberian Seven

Timothy Chmykhalov with Danny Smith

The plight of the 'Siberian Seven' attracted widespread publicity and support.

Timothy Chmykhalov, youngest member of the seven, vividly recounts the events leading to the entry into the US Embassy in 1978, the long years of hoping and waiting, the uncertainty which faced them when they left in 1983 and finally the freedom which they found in America.

Release is a powerful testimony of faith and courage amidst intense pressure and threat of persecution. A story of hope and determination in the face of much discouragement.

NOW I CALL HIM BROTHER

Alec Smith

Alec Smith, son of Ian Smith the rebel Prime Minister of Rhodesia whose Unilateral Declaration of Independence plunged his country into twelve years of bloody racial war, has written his own story of those years.

The story of his life takes him from early years of rebellion against his role as 'Ian Smith's son' through his youth as a drop-out, hippy and drug peddler into the Rhodesian forces.

A dramatic Christian conversion experience at the height of the civil war transformed his life and led to the passionate conviction to see reconciliation and peace in a deeply divided country.

What follows is a thrilling account of how God can take a dedicated life and help to change the course of history.

OUT OF THE MELTING POT

Bob Gordon

Faith does not operate in a vacuum, it operates in human lives. God wants your life to be a crucible of faith.

Bob Gordon draws together Biblical principles and personal experience to provide valuable insights into this key area. Particular reference is made to the lessons he leant recently as God provided £600,000 to buy Roffey Place Christian Training Centre.

Out of the Melting Pot is Bob Gordon's powerful testimony to the work of God today and a profound challenge to shallow views of faith.

If you wish to receive *regular information* about *new books*, please send your name and address to:

London Bible Warehouse
PO Box 123
Basingstoke
Hants RG23 7NL

Name...

Address ....

....

....

....

I am especially interested in:
☐ Biographies
☐ Fiction
☐ Christian living
☐ Issue related books
☐ Academic books
☐ Bible study aids
☐ Children's books
☐ Music
☐ Other subjects

P.S. If you have ideas for new Christian Books or other products, please write to us too!